Killing America

Killing America

The Invisible War

William Davidson

Copyright © 2016 by William Davidson.

Library of Congress Control Number:		2016914125
ISBN:	Hardcover	978-1-5245-3838-5
	Softcover	978-1-5245-3837-8
	eBook	978-1-5245-3836-1

All rights reserved. No part of this book may be reproduced or transmitted in any form or by any means, electronic or mechanical, including photocopying, recording, or by any information storage and retrieval system, without permission in writing from the copyright owner.

Any people depicted in stock imagery provided by Thinkstock are models, and such images are being used for illustrative purposes only. Certain stock imagery © Thinkstock.

Print information available on the last page.

Rev. date: 10/25/2016

To order additional copies of this book, contact:
Xlibris
1-888-795-4274
www.Xlibris.com
Orders@Xlibris.com
746609

Contents

Overview vii
Chapter 1 1
Chapter 2 11
Chapter 3 15
Chapter 4 29
Chapter 5 43
Chapter 6 57
Chapter 7 73
Chapter 8 85
Chapter 9 99
Chapter 10 113
Chapter 11 127
Chapter 12 141
Chapter 13 147
Chapter 14 151
Summary 219

OVERVIEW

THERE IS AN invisible war raging in the United States. Big business, foreign governments, organized crime, and political special interests have been joined by radical Islamic groups that have infiltrated our legislative branch through lobbyists. They are tampering with and changing our laws! These changes have brought our system to a halt and opened our vaults to theft at a catastrophic level.

Our legal system is destroying the American family while filling our prisons. Drug cartels and drug lords are filling our streets with dope. Islamic Jihadists are blending into our population and infiltrating our infrastructure. Conflict and dissention are being stirred up and enflamed from behind the scenes by our enemies. Wedges of division are being driven into our population between, race, gender, class, and the police and government. Just about every type of thief, opportunist, and enemy have descended upon us like a swarm of locust.

Psychological warfare tactics have been used by everyone from the common thief to the globalists in America says former Marine Corps Chief Scout, William Davidson as he pulls the veil off CIA tactics and military strategies to expose the invisible war that is killing America.

With electronic warfare being waged over the internet in cyber space, chemical warfare being waged with drugs on our streets, and psychological warfare being waged on our leaders, we are being robbed blind of our money, technology, and secrets. At the same time the tampered with laws have damaged our system and institutions to where each day of operation causes even more financial destruction. The daily conflict and theft is used with the sleight of hand to distract us while we are attacked with invisible forces.

Davidson acts as our Chief Scout and puts a finger on each attacking force, the damage done, the tactics used, and the overall strategies. Davidson steps up as a tactician and calls on the nation to pull together as one. We need to attack 9 parts of our economy simultaneously to stop the destruction of the United States. The 9 Part Plan requiring blocks or sections of our system and its work force be picked up and moved like the pieces on a chess board. Damage from our tampered with system will stop and enhanced security and wealth will return to Americans from all walks of life this is your call to action. Join together, call our leaders to stop the madness and save America.

CHAPTER 1

So let's sit down and pretend we are an Al-Qaeda Intel branch. Now let's look at some of the information they may have collected and see what kind of operations they may have going on.

I wonder if they saw how to use lobbyist to make or stop new laws. They could even use deception tactics to fund lobbies without them knowing.

Let's take a second to look at everyone that is attacking America with invisible tactics. Besides Islamic fanatics, you have some foreign governments, greedy businessmen, cartels and other criminal groups, special interest groups, and all those that are destroying America or robbing us or profiteering.

Now back to someone like Al-Qaeda. What would a chemical attack from them look like? 1. US dollars to Arab oil purchase, 2. Arab oil money under the table to drug cartels supplying America! Bingo!

While the US military is looking for missiles with nerve agents for a chemical attack on us, a new type of chemical attack slips under the radar.

Now if I had masterminded a sneak attack on American shores with an agent that was invisible to America's military defenses, what would I do to exploit the success of the attack?

If I had watched how the US car insurance companies used lawmakers through lobbies to line their pockets at the tax payer's expense, I could setup just as brilliant of a plan as the insurance companies did when they got the seat belt law passed. The insurance companies stayed in the shadows, funded groups like state patrols and child care groups, and the lobbyist did a nationwide commercial campaign to save children's lives by wearing seat belts. Well that did not have to be a law. A public awareness campaign would have been sufficient. Just like public awareness has brought down cigarette use. But the insurance companies needed hard numbers on their financial reports for stockholders and potential future sales. Their biggest expense was bodily injury. Now, the public taxpayers pay police departments to make sure the insurance companies expenses are lower and their stock prices higher! How slick was that.

So if Al-Qaeda and similar groups are funneling money to drug cartels that supply the United States, what can they do to enhance the damage to the US?

So far, US dollars financed the attack on us by purchasing oil from our two-faced enemy. Then US dollars were siphoned out of our economy to buy the illegal drugs. Say 10 percent civilian casualties from drug addiction. Then US tax dollars were used for extra prisons, drug rehabilitation, and welfare for the families that lost breadwinners! A pretty good strike on American soil and its spreading with Afghan heroin.

The next step would be to get the Americans to persecute the people who get addicted. That's where the lobbyist come in. Support harsher drug laws. All the groups that hire lobbyists are not paying close enough attention to where they get their money from. It's easy for foreign enemies to fund special interest groups without them being aware.

Let's go back to foreign enemies deliberately planning to attack America and prong #1 of the attack is to finance drug traffickers for a chemical attack.

Prong #2 – Cause financial damage to America by hiring lobbyists to change their laws to waste their money.

Prong #3 – Use the Internet to hack into soft civilian financial targets.

Prong #4 – Destroy the character of the people, make Americans look like low-life scum.

Prong #5 – Destroy their relationships with friendly foreign powers.

This is how we would attack someone. There would be several prongs and multiple waves.

I believe there are several more areas that are being attacked, but I need to talk about hiring lobbyists. I believe foreign enemies, criminals, and special interest groups have infiltrated our system through the lawmaking corridor and are blocking laws that are good for the nation and backing laws that are for corrupt reasons. I believe this tampering with the laws has had many unforeseen consequences as unneeded laws enter to support a special interest need. The new laws intertwine and collide with necessary laws causing several problems that affect a streamline cost-effective operation for each special interest law put on the books.

Your special interest is destroying America; each time you tamper with the making of a law, you get several bonus problems.

Bin Laden's people were over here in the nineties, going to our schools and studying us. I was in Lebanon in the early 80s and heard that the Muslim extremists didn't care if it took a thousand years to destroy us as I picked through the ruble of the Marine Barracks in Beirut. It had just been leveled by a suicide bomber.

I believe in their conviction; I saw it firsthand several times. So if the tampering with our system from radical Muslims started in the 90s, let's make a quick comparison of America's efficiency in present day warfare. The United States decimated the fourth largest army in the world in a couple days in 1991.

Now today, our military seems ineffective and unable to accomplish or reach its goals! The men in the US Military are better equipped and trained than the 1991 forces. Could it be that our system has been secretly tampered with? And we can't do anything without getting buried in litigation. I think that's what I call too many laws in the way to get anything done.

If radical Muslims want to bring us to our knees to destroy us, they have to break us financially. So let's say they are attacking and call this phase one of the Invisible War against America. So we have to assume they are showing all our weaknesses to all groups interested in plundering the United States of its riches. Then they will be recruiting and funding criminal organizations and criminals within enemy foreign governments to steal from us.

They must also divide us, so I will mention how I believe the police agencies are being turned against the civilian population and the civilian population is being turned against the government. But for now, I'm going back to the hiring of lobbyists. Infiltration of our system by secretly funding lobbyists to pass harmful laws while disinformation and distraction campaigns keep us busy sorting out the facts. Special interests persuade lawmakers to push harder to pass something foreign analysts have calculated the damage to our economy on already.

Let's look at MADD (Mothers Against Drunk Drivers) lobbying group. They have become the financially largest lobbying organization we have. I brought them up because I looked up online who their donors were.

There were plenty of Islamic or Muslim groups on that list. It would be easy for American enemies to secretly help fund that organization.

But why would they? How about beer drinking being one of America's biggest national past times? From an enemy intelligence report on the United States, it would read:

"The backbone of America's favorite drink is beer. Soldiers, construction workers, and competitive sports athletes and fans have a strong love for beer drinking. We should support more and tougher laws on drinking as that would affect their providers and fighting class of people."

If foreign enemies have been tampering with DWI laws, boy they have scored a big win for breaking America financially.

A quick look at a combined effort with different tactics.

Persuasion – it would be easy to use psychological warfare tactics on distraught mothers who have lost children to drunk drivers.

Fund them with enemy money while they are grief-stricken, and they would never know.

Blind voters and lawmakers with false numbers on statistics. No one would even think to check.

Hide the truth about cost and damage to civilian families and the dollar cost to our nation. With a smoke screen put up with excessive information. And what do you have? An invisible strike against the backbone of our nation? I can show the most common false information used in this tactic to damage our nation. The 0.08 BAC issued to determine drunk. So 0.08 BAC equals "drunk."

This is false information. Let me bring a few things to light in case you have never used alcohol. In nationwide alcohol education classes, three mixed drinks or three beers is enough alcohol to bring a 200 lb. man to a 0.08 BAC. I am a two-hundred-pound man and when I have had three drinks, that is when I start feeling the effects of alcohol. Or in layman's terms, you start to catch a buzz. I have asked people around the nation if they are drunk after three drinks. The answer is unanimously *no*!

People started noticing that we had made a mistake setting the BAC at 0.08 equals "drunk" (or as I contend possibly been tricked). So whether it was a mistake or a trick, it was covered up. So a smoke screen was initiated and an education program implemented or (brain washing) to change from drunk driving to impaired driving. So now, what was a legitimate problem initially is being used to destroy and jail anyone who uses alcohol. Let me pull the veil off impaired driving and expose impaired driving for what it is.

Your driving is impaired at night! Your driving is impaired at sunrise or sunset if you're driving east or west! Your driving is impaired in high winds or rains! Your driving is impaired while driving on snow or ice! Your driving is impaired during heavy snowfall or fog! Should we be jailed for driving in these conditions? At 0.08, you are only slightly impaired, and if you are stopped enough times for it, you can get life in prison.

It's a facade. We see it every day but do not recognize it as an enemy strike against America in an invisible war. Let's look at the damage. It's catastrophic. Our prisons are filling up with working class and fighting class men for the most part. Their families fall into poverty. Welfare and public assistance are draining taxpayer's dollars. Not to mention additional prisons draining tax dollars.

These burdens on taxpayers are causing a riff between the people and the government over having to raise taxes. While illegals and foreigners are moving in to take the jobs of our working class while they do prison sentences, they are barred from good jobs because of either felony status or what is called a criminal record.

Then we have a disgruntled group of working and fighting class men to recruit what are being called homegrown terrorist. These men are as easy to persuade or manipulate as the distraught mothers who had lost children I talked about in the MADD. organization.

Wow! What a multidirectional strike.

It's easy to see why things like this have gotten so out of control.

MADD is powerful enough to get people voted in or out of public office just as easily as they can affect a change. Here is an example of what happens to our system when special interest groups get someone voted in or out to support a special interest. They don't know which way to vote on other more serious matters and then fall into bipartisanship lines and join the gridlock of Democrat against Republican voting. And nothing gets done.

My intentions are not to blame or downgrade a group like MADD which sprung up from noble intentions. I was trying to show how diverse the damage from one bad change in our legal system can be.

Although damage from drugs and alcohol parallel the same lines, I believe they came to us from different tactics being used to try to destroy America.

CHAPTER 2

A CHEMICAL ATTACK AND a System Infiltration.

Both of these attacks, I think, were designed to drain both money and manpower from our defense capability.

Then once they gain success, it becomes easy to exploit the successes simply by the power of suggestion.

These two attacks alone are enough to destroy America, given enough time. And with our system having been changed so many times and so many special interest personnel put in office, it's difficult to see what's wrong much less fix it. Even though people see the problems, they can't use the system to fix the problems.

As soon as someone makes a move to fix something, the people who broke it move to defend it while enemies to our nation who have infiltrated or learned how to manipulate from abroad attack those who would initiate the repair.

Here is what the invisible attacks look like. A smoke screen of disinformation and clutter is put up to hide the problem from average citizens. Then smear campaigns and character assassination are executed on those who try to fix a problem with the system. Then tampered with laws will be used to bury the problem in litigation.

It won't take long and most people won't even know what the problem was. With these tactics, the strike becomes invisible to average people and after some time even to the trained eye.

With average people not able to see the problem, they are able to be used.

An enemy intelligence report would read: Americans are competitive in the work area; they strive to be better, work harder, and produce more than their coworkers.

American exceptionalism in the workplace is what made America a great power.

Now with their system infiltrated, we can use American exceptionalism to have Americans destroy America faster than ever.

Let's look at judges and prosecutors and police departments. It's fair to say the people that fill these positions are some of our finer and more sought after caliber of people.

These types of jobs are also public service which also draws a type of people that want to help. So we have assembled some of the best workers we can that thrive on exceptional performance and a desire to stand out among their peers as the best at what they do.

Combine this with a legal system that has been tampered with infiltrated and can be manipulated.

This is what it looks like to the public servants sent out to fight the war on drugs and save innocent families from being slaughtered by drunk drivers.

The judges, prosecutors, and state patrols are hauling drug criminals and wanton drunk drivers out to slaughter innocent families by the truck load. Then they are put away in prisons as long as the law allows. Each of these public servants striving to outdo the other! Well, most of the drug criminals operate from outside the United States, and the majority of people brought in on drug charges are the addicts while the majority of the criminals go free! At the same time, the state patrol is bringing in all drivers they encounter that have been drinking as drunk drivers. They think they are doing their job. Not helping to destroy America.

CHAPTER 3

THE PUBLIC SERVANTS' hands are tied. The system they are part of contains the laws that special interest groups changed and foreign enemies and criminal enterprises interfered with to allow them to rob us and make us waste so much money that we can't maintain our superpower status.

Police agencies in the United States have been reduced to law enforcement personnel. Well, who is stopping crime? Real crime! Sheriffs, marshals, rangers, deputies, and patrolmen are all busy doing law enforcement. The public, through the power of persuasion (brainwashing), has named breaking these new laws that are contaminated with ulterior motives as criminal behavior.

So what happened to what used to be criminal? Like rape, robbery, stealing, child molestation, thuggery, murder, and so on. This was a criminal behavior when I was younger. If someone reports what was a crime when I was younger, something would be done. Today the men being paid to protect us are too busy enforcing laws. Who is protecting us? It's mostly civilian men. Nobody trusts the police because if you call them for help, half of your family or friends may be arrested for breaking a law. What I call a criminal though will call the law to get protection when the man of the house or protector of the family is after someone that has wronged his group criminally. Thieves will call in on someone for drinking and driving, so they can rob them while they are in jail.

God help the people addicted to illegal drugs. They suffer the most horrendous crimes. Criminals will weigh what an addict will not report based on how afraid of what the police or courts will charge the addict with if they call them for help. So they accept rapes and beatings as less punishment than a drug conviction. Here is what government level foreign enemies want to see, public fear of the police. In the history of revolutions, this is a step in the right direction. Foreign enemies need to see the United States have a revolution. In our weakened financial state, you can bet the next step in the invisible war against us will be to persuade us to fight among ourselves.

For now, let's get back to law enforcement and our legal system.

I think this is where we can start to unveil the invisible damage done to our system and people. It is the judges, prosecutors, and police that can expose the laws that are costing us money on several fronts and not helping or protecting the people. This is also like a dividing line in our nation where the federal government, the financial elite, the business leaders, and leaders of science and education can't see below. What I mean is the middle and lower class. The leaders of our nation are just as susceptible to the invisible warfare tactics as we are. And because of their financial power and higher education, they are not likely to see what is going on below the middle class. That is the majority of our nation, and it is hell fire under attack. Don't get me wrong. The elite are under attack also. But they know it. The CIA, NSA, FBI are working on it at their level. They know our infrastructure is under attack, but it appears most of their focus is overseas. Nobody is looking at our two hundred-year-old system, and the gaping holes that high-tech enemies can come right in and sabotage at will. No one is putting the spotlight on the psychological tactics used to screw up our system because all of our elite are using them on each other. CNN and FOX, along with other investigative news crew, report on these psychological tactics regularly. They report covert operations overseas and at the highest levels of government.

They don't seem to be connecting who persuaded or deceived a special interest group or lawmaker to stop or install a law that is financially problematic or causing chaos inside our own country. We can project what the side effects of a law change will be ahead of time just the same as a foreign analyst studying us can. Our investigative reporters should be able to track where the money and ideas came from that manipulated someone in charge to take part in a system change that harmed us as a nation by wasting taxpayer's dollars or opening an infiltration or robbery route or just causing slowing or clogging of daily operations.

They can and do find the damage and report on it. But it doesn't seem to get connected all the way to the beginning, so we cannot see if the problem was just a blind buffoon or idiot. Or a criminal that sets something up to steal a few million and caused hundreds of millions in damage. Then again, maybe the blind idiot was manipulated by an enemy of the nation and funded by a third or fourth party away from the crime. That would be very hard to track or prove. But that's what we have to look for if we are going to solve the problem.

Here is a question I have heard on a national news report. What is behind the fact that more police officers have been shot in the last year or two than in the entire combined history of our country. The police shootings are random and unconnected.

The reports do not have an answer. This is what I think. If there is an effort by foreign enemies to drive a wedge between the people and law enforcement and the people and government. Here is a sign of it. I will show the big companies like FOX and so forth where the trail is to answer this question. FOX and other investigative reporters are the financially elite, a class that does not live or work in the areas that the evidence trail starts as to why so many police are being shot in America today. It would be easy to put some labels on it like revenge or fear. Fear of what? The damage that could be caused by a simple courtesy stop to inform someone of a taillight being out. So let's say we have a state trooper thinking he will do a favor and tell a citizen his light is out. The man driving the vehicle is on his way home from work with a big overtime paycheck after a sixteen-hour worked day. Trooper pulls him over; the man shoots and kills the trooper. Next day, the paper reads felon with long criminal history kills state trooper. Well, the truth of the matter could have been the man was a hard working loving father and devoted husband that was an alcoholic. Let's say a responsible alcoholic, a three to six beer a day man. Rarely, if ever, does he drink until he is drunk. If he killed a police officer, it's probably because he may have been facing a very long prison sentence for having beer on his breath while on probation, maybe no driver's license.

This man could have been facing losing his family's home. He may have lost another home prior to this one. He probably spent his children's college fund on legal bills. He probably has no retirement fund either. This does not justify murder. And an event like this would be tragic. Our prisons are full of men who did not kill the trooper. I have also heard many conversations in construction crowds where men are preparing plans to fight or run if anymore law enforcement personnel try to stop them for anything. Let's remember we are trying to track down who is responsible for so many police officers being shot. I remember a case where someone opened fire on a coffee shop where local police had their coffee. Obviously revenge! The plot to drive a wedge between civilian and law enforcement is showing its ugly little head here in our hunt to find out why so many police are being shot. So this is finding its way back to lobbyist like MADD and other lawmakers. Let's look at court orders. It's the law that you have to follow them. Are they laws? Where do they come from? What makes them legal? Is it an oxymoron to court order an alcoholic or addict not to drink or drug?

Almost every case in courts involving alcoholic/addicts has additional charges on them pertaining to violations of court orders not to drink or drug.

It seems that the problem with addictions is you can't just stop when you want to. So how is a court order going to work? So the public servants seem to be getting shot for enforcing the laws.

Now we are right back to our system being infiltrated and tampered with by secret invisible tactics. So government level foreign enemy, criminal organizations, business, and special interest groups are responsible for the amount of police officers being shot in the United States. If all our investigative reporters turned their resources toward following the money that goes to lobbyist and the people who influence them, we could put specific names on who is responsible for each area of damage. A more important thought would be to close that hole that damage is pouring into our system from. The major damage to our nation is being done at the executive level of our government and the law enforcement and judicial level. The courts that are administrating punishment to the public on behalf of the law enforcement agencies is where the dividing lines of the rich or upper-class and the poor and middle class is at. The executive level government leaders from the upper-class cannot see past the level of the judges and police. The financially powerful are in the upper-class also. They too cannot see past the courts and law enforcers. The rich also pay most of the taxes and can't see what is happening to the middle class and poor. And that is they are not paying taxes because their lives and families are being destroyed by the corrupted laws, and the taxes are being raised to build prisons and imprison them.

And to make things worse, scavengers are building businesses off the destroyed families and the imprisoned population which is going to make it harder to repair the system as the scavenging entrepreneurs will lobby not to give up their captive clients. Just as the upper-class cannot see past the judicial system.

The vast majority of our population, the lower and middle class, can't see past the law enforcement and judicial systems looking toward the upper-class executive government leaders. All they see is smoke and mirrors. There is so much disinformation and lying we can't even vote for the right person or even get the right people to vote for. I would draw the battle lines for the invisible war against America at the district and superior courts. The judges and prosecutors have access to the records that could show some major financial damage to our nation. Basically, we need to pull the veils off the damage and add it up. We would need law enforcement personnel to return to being public servants. Our tax dollars pay them. What happened to "serve and protect?"

How about "crime stoppers?" Laws have tied the hands of the police to stop crime before it happens. Their job has been twisted from "serve and protect" to law enforcement by contaminated laws that allow organized criminals to control what they do simply by lobbying for laws to protect them while they run circles around our crime stoppers making them go enforce laws against us, the people these criminals are feeding on. This law enforcement thing has alienated the public from the police. The sight of a police vehicle on the side of the road or in your rearview mirror strikes fear into most of the civilian population. No one wants to talk to them either for fear that what they say could be used in any other of several contexts other than the context it was intended for. So we have a police force the public is afraid to ask for help. Organized crime gets lobbyists and lawyers to build laws around their types of crime to bar the police from interfering. We need an executive order from the president for the police to shut down all known drug houses. Every city and town in the United States is allowing known drug houses to operate. The premise is that if they watch them, they will catch the big dealers. Well, who gave them that bright idea? The cartel members that infiltrated our drug enforcement agencies? KGB? North Koreans? Leaving a drug house open is like opening a valve to release poison gas into our cities. And a vacuum hose to suck money out of our cities. So the longer you leave it open, the farther the poison gas spreads and the more money gets sucked out of the economy. Maybe they get a big dealer once in a while. But the damage to the community is catastrophic and widespread.

Being a combat marine veteran medical care has been a big part of my training and education. As I mentioned earlier, I was fresh out of a war zone and found myself in Washington State looking at a meth epidemic. I mentioned it to a doctor and asked how to treat it. He said if someone takes meth, it is a medical emergency and nothing can be done until the person has been detoxed.

Well I find that to be a fairly true statement. This brings to mind our system. I see the possibility of more damage from tampering. I see the courts trying to implement recovery programs. This seems like a job for the medical industry not the penal system? The way things are going looks like our system is broken and is sucking our people into our prison system and spitting them out into the public assistance network, stripped of their gun rights by felony statutes and now unqualified for higher paying jobs. This is going on in the middle and lower class. Remember the upper-class can't see this as they are not as susceptible to the problems because of money.

I think they would be interested in the upper-class as it is their tax dollars being wasted to fund it.

Our military which is second to none, sits dormant. While China, North Korea, Russia, and Iran steal our technology and secrets so they can catch up militarily. Now countries like these have infiltrated government and corporate positions for more than fifty years, so they can infiltrate our CIA through US Government positions or corporate positions to avoid the intense background investigation they would endure if they were CIA foreign hires. Granted there is colossal theft and waste going on at the top, but it seems everyone knows about that. I think the loss at the bottom is just as devastating as the amount of money lost at the top. And at the top is being lost also the trust of our longtime allies because we are being made to look so incompetent. I'm going to get into some of the invisible damage at the top a little later because so many news agencies are covering parts of that. It also should be pieced together, so we can see how all the invisible strikes link together at the top as in the bottom. But the war at the middle and lower class is where I live, and the part of the damage the war on America has kept invisible. So let's look at moral decay and character of Americans. We are being made to look despicable abroad and a lot of it is self-inflicted. Let's compare 1990–2014. I believe now we have more people in prison in the United States than all other major countries combined have. Let's take a look at the effects of imprisoning the working and fighting class men for drug and alcohol addictions. Most of these men are just your average family men. Two-thirds of our prison populations are comprised of these types of men. The other third are predatory thugs that have spent most of their life behind bars lifting weights and tattooing their bodies. So there are some issues! When working men get thrown in prison, they become "prey."

They will encounter being robbed, beaten, disrespected, and possibly sexually assaulted. With the evolution in society over the last twenty-five years, gay behavior has become acceptable but not average or normal in most Americans lives. So if you are not confined and do not want to be in a homosexual environment, you don't have to be. In our prisons, you don't have a choice. Prisons are breeding grounds for creating sexually sick people. So you can see that if you throw a normal family man in this environment after he loses his job, home, vehicle, and possibly his family for consuming a few beers. He may never be right again. When he walks back into society, he takes with him an education on how to be a criminal. Maybe thoughts of revenge. Possibly sexually deviant behavior. Sounds like the makings of a homegrown terrorist or cop killer. Besides the financial drain on our country, distraction of families, now we have turned a family man into a burden on society. If I were a trained intelligence agent against the United States and I was involved in a plan to secretly support all laws that imprison Americans and its working beautifully and is now on autopilot, I can turn my attention to exploiting the success.

Don't think this is far-fetched. This is how our own CIA works. So don't think we are not deeply infiltrated by enemies that are well-funded and have their hands in everything that will damage us or profit them.

CHAPTER 4

LET'S LOOK AT the image of Americans abroad. Rest assured this is very important. To an enemy, we must be made to look like scum that's for two very important reasons. One, so our enemies can recruit help against us in a time of war. And two, so no one would want to assist us in a time of war. One of the best tools that are being used to destroy the image of Americans is the prison system. Besides being called an ex-con, felon, or criminal, you're a burden on society with possibly no job, place to live, transportation, or driver's license. And depending on how long you were in, possibly a sexual deviant or sexual predator. This is one way we are being portrayed overseas. The prisons are also releasing animals of the worst kind imaginable. These are men incarcerated for twenty to thirty years that are predatory thugs of the worst imaginable intentions. Look on the milk cartons and missing person's lists. Probably 90 percent of those missing are dead, most likely from sexual predators made in our very own prisons. There are foreign news agencies reporting on these types of things in every area that our foreign friends and enemies will hear them in their daily news; special interest groups, government leaders, and Hollywood celebrities are some of the easiest to manipulate.

Enemy intelligence personnel look for any conflict in our country that makes us look bad abroad. Then they find a way to incite problems that will flare up a conflict and put it or keep it in the news. I'll give you a couple scenarios as to what I would do in the United States to make headlines that show moral decay in the fabric of our character. The USA represented religious freedom in an old school lifestyle based on traditional Christian values. This is what made long-lasting devout friendships between us and many of our allies. Now we are depicted as a nation of criminals that have turned homosexual and or into pedophiles spreading pornography around the world. As an enemy plotting war against the United States, I would use the homosexual or gay angle to make the United States look less formidable to conservative armies or Muslim extremists. First I would contact Hollywood celebrities and rattle up some gay rights anxiety. It would only take one famous gay actor. Then find a politician that needed help getting voted in. Now we have a big public gay rights controversy all over the papers. So here we go again with special interest groups, funding lobbyist, and putting in another group of politicians with an agenda of gay rights instead of fixing America. In reality, enemies of our nation needed to give America a look that is not as fierce when you're contemplating facing them on the battlefield. Now we have American exceptionalism going into overdrive! Now mind you, I know what human rights are. Do gays have special rights? Or do we just all have the same rights?

On a personal note, most people don't want to know what is going on in your bedroom. In average homes, it's considered rude or inconsiderate to discuss those matters openly. And if there are children around, it's just plain wrong!

So what better ways to show moderate Muslims what Americans are like? That is if your religion has been hijacked by extremists, and you're trying to raise support against America. Now American is not gay. A very small portion of Americans are gay. But Americans are compassionate and accepting. The Islamic countries in which armies are being solicited to kill Americans do not tolerate homosexuality. In some countries, it's punishable by death. That's where suicide bombers are being recruited. So it would be in the best interest of the United States to be discreet about matters such as tolerance for gays while at war in an area where people would view us as trash for our tolerance.

But instead, with a little help from enemy agents, gay activists light up the headlines giving foreign enemy military a little more confidence that they may be facing sissy la-la boys when facing US military. Don't take offense to the gay slur as that is the typical view of gay men. This is true in America also but political correctness is settling in. Most heterosexuals have cleaned up there language and keep their opinions to themselves, in defense of gays that I have known. They have been discreet and very respectful especially around families. For the most part, they would rather be the loud flamboyant gays and left alone as they just want to blend in. I'll get back to how I would use gay Americans in the war against America. Use the public platform Hollywood celebrities have by manipulating them into rushing to the aid of gays rights. Get them to fund lobbyist make more or change more laws to clog the system. Help get people in and out of office to support a gay agenda instead of an American agenda. It could not have come at a worse time. As the US headlines read about gay marriages, President Obama pencils flamboyant gays into the military. The jihadist gets emboldened as a lot of

American hard corps fighting men distances themselves from the military. So we have enemies of the nation manipulating the image of Americans abroad while at the same time damage the system and weaken the military while giving enemy combatants the courage to strike at our military. Now, that was just one attempt to exploit success in invisible strikes against America. So that brings up President Obama using CIA tactics to get reelected while at the same time CIA tactics are being used on him by foreign enemies to bring America to its knees financially.

"They say time reveals everything." As its 2014 while I'm writing this, Obama is still in office and we will have to wait and let history show us if Obama is an enemy to the United States, a criminal, or just blind and naive as an innocent child. Right now, I'm leaning toward a Chicago style organized criminal history for Obama. With a naive streak a mile wide! It's painfully obvious when Obama uses CIA tactics on the public, such as lying, disinformation, and manipulation. He is so bad at using these tactics that it is an international embarrassment. Every time he tries, FOX news exposes the disinformation. Then Obama uses Chicago Style thuggery to take our money and give it to people that are making it disappear! And of course, that crack in our system that foreign enemies use is being used by the Obama Administration to write laws to protect the criminals that kidnapped our president. So our president is so involved in trying to payback all the favors he owed for help getting in office that he has no idea of the damage that he has caused. Not to mention all of our international friends are watching our enemies trick and manipulate the president's administration with the same tactics that he tries to use so ineffectively. It is no wonder that our president's staff can't see what is going on below the middle class. They are being bombarded with disinformation being manipulated, lied to, tricked, coerced; every type of treacherous psychological tactic known to man is being used against our leaders.

We have some pretty sneaky business giants that are in the mix right at the top with our worst enemies. Pharmaceutical companies use psyops to manipulate our leaders just like our enemies do. They spend millions hiding information that would keep people from having to use their product. They also infiltrate our government positions so they can regulate or facilitate drug sales or use to benefit their companies. Let's look at President Obama's election. With key timing while blatantly smearing Mitt Romney, false employment numbers were posted one week before the election. Hispanic voters were being persuaded by immigration lies, and Obama penciled in homosexuals to the military.

These are typical Chicago style tactics! But I think it goes a lot farther than Obama's reelection team. Let's look at how many groups needed Obama reelected. Most people would say all US enemies as it is already obvious that Obama is a weak president. If I were an intelligence network working against the United States, I would help Obama shut down US oil production. So that means Arab oil-producing countries get to keep selling oil to the United States. Since US oil companies fund predominately conservative republicans, I would say Arabs helped fund Obama and manipulated him into using his power to affect US oil company profits, so they would have less money to support opposition to his presidency. We can throw in jihadists and terrorist groups also as they get most of their money from Arab or Muslim oil sales. Obviously, the North Koreans, Chinese, and Russians had their money and effort in there somewhere. They have gotten a big payoff in that US power and influence abroad in rapid decline.

Let's look a little closer to home to see who might be using invisible tactics against Obama. How about the pharmaceutical companies and the rest of the medical industry and the insurance companies? These groups have been inundated with fraud and thieves lining up to siphon off as much of the US's money as they can get through the Affordable Health Care Act. What I wouldn't give to know who influenced the president to start this catastrophic theft. Even though all the American companies that stand to gain the most, or the opportunists looking to line their pockets are suspect. I would look past them to the jihad types that would use persuasion or manipulation tactics on the opportunists just to use their greed as another instrument in setting up a financial collapse of the United States.

The giant food companies are an instrument related to the pharmaceutical companies and the Affordable Health Care Act. Let me make the connection real quick, then we will talk about it in a little more detail.

Our food companies are hiding nutritional facts that require us to have pharmaceutical companies and health care! This is a big one, and if I'm aware of it, you can be sure that intelligence collection assets from our enemies are aware of it also.

The same tactics that the CIA and KGB use are being used to cover-up this information. So I have to suspect that the food companies' public relations and advertising have been infiltrated and supported by enemies of our nation. Our food companies also infiltrate and manipulate government positions. The reason is simple. Information on nutrition is advancing as fast as computer technology. Well, everyone has heard to eat more fresh fruits and vegetables. That's just a smoke screen made out of one sentence of truth that is repeated so many ways by so many groups that the subject is flooded with information so bad that the whole truth is buried. In a nutshell, the food in the United States that is being sold in stores or restaurants is nutritionally depleted. The more it is cooked and the longer it is stored, the less nutritional value it will have. This is monumental in the destruction of the United States. That is because our diet leads straight to prescription medicine and hospitalization. Remember how much money is being wasted and siphoned off below the middle class? Now this waste is going on in all classes of society. In addition to how bad processed foods are. The facts about how to get proper nutrition are being covered up. A lot of people have an interest in hiding these facts besides our enemies.

Let me lay out some nutritional information to connect the dots. The average American consumes a large dump truck load of each of these nutritionally dead products in their life: sugar, flour, and salt. Don't believe the advertisements on the labels either. The federal government ordered that flour be enriched with vitamins because it was void of any vitamins. Sugar doesn't give you energy; it releases the energy your body stores for emergency needs. This is a lot of junk to process through your body. Here's the problem. A cooked meal takes four to six hours to digest. Since the meal is cooked, any live food enzymes that aid in digestion are destroyed. Your body has to supply all the energy for digestion. That is why we want to take a nap after a big meal. On the other hand, a meal of raw fruits and vegetables will be digested in about twenty minutes with minimal energy expended as the live plant enzymes aid in breaking down the meal. So that brings us to the miles of lymph nodes in our bodies which act as the janitorial corridors that run through bone, muscle, fat, and skin. By the time digestion is complete, energy levels are too low for cleaning. All the carcinogens and additives in our food are getting left in our flesh polluting our bodies. Then given enough time, we start getting sick and diseased.

What it amounts to is two out of three Americans will die of some kind of sickness or disease because of our diet. So health care is not going to get cheaper by passing an Affordable Health Care Act. So how did this happen? The biggest robbery in US history? Did foreign enemies whisper in the ears of our leaders to guide them into a catastrophic waste? Or was health care used to draw voters to a cause? You can see there are a lot of enemies, thieves, and frauds that would have tried to manipulate this waste either to profit from or just to misguide us. If I was an Al-Qaeda or North Korean, I would be helping the pharmaceutical and food companies cover-up or discredit the flow of new information on vitamins, minerals, diet, and nutrition. It's this information we need to reduce health care costs. And the big prescription drug and food companies don't want this information out as much as our enemies don't. For our enemies, we are eating ourselves to death. And for the drug companies, they are taking our money for prescriptions before we die. The bottom-line so far on health care is we have to "eat closer to the vine." What that means is a fruit or vegetable starts deteriorating in its nutritional value of vitamins and minerals the day it is picked. Heat from cooking really depreciates the value. Then other processing and storage really kills the value of the food. Our bodies have to work hard to extract any nutrition from what we are eating. Our diet is consuming our life's energy in digestion leaving our bodies clogged with truckloads of worthless food that has got to be processed through our bodies.

Well here is the key. Raw fruits and vegetables and fasting clean our bodies. The digestive enzymes consumed in live food leave your bodies' energy to do its other functions including cleaning and repair at the cellular level. There are health experts that are healing people through their diets. Therapeutic doses of vitamins and minerals are bringing people back to good health. This is not what prescription drug companies want to hear. Almost every minimum daily requirement for vitamins and minerals set by the federal food and drug administration was corrupted by the giant food companies. The processed foods were discovered to have little, if any, vitamin and mineral content left in them. So they bribed the FDA officials or manipulated or coerced them into setting the standards as low as you could without getting ill. That's where therapeutic doses of vitamins and minerals are being used to heal sick people. Usually, the vitamins are given thousands of times higher than the minimum that were set by the FDA, so it would be legal to sell some of the food in stores that we are buying.

Don't believe the advertisements on the new enriched vitamin packed products; they were the ones that were going to be banned if the food companies didn't add some vitamin content to them.

Milk is not a good source of calcium. The molecules of cows' cells are so much bigger than human cells; it is difficult for our bodies to absorb them. Vitamin D was added to milk as a government order at the same time flour was ordered to be enriched; that was the easiest way to get vitamin supplements to the widespread impoverished portion of the United States.

So our best investment for affordable health care is a vegetable garden and fruit trees for every home in America. Civilians could have done that without government money!

It sounds pretty low-tech, but I would bet we could build a plan around education and eating closer to the vine that would cut health care costs dramatically given a few years. Not to mention saving our lifesavings, we spend to die from a horrible disease. Instead of dying at home in bed of natural causes. Well even if President Obama uses Chicago style organized crime tactics, it seems that he has been manipulated and tricked by outside forces to become unproductive and cripple our economy.

To be fair to Obama, basically, his pants were pulled down by the FOX news people and his weaknesses were exposed. That made him a target for psyops experts from all walks of life.

It also reminds me of when President Bush Jr. sent troops back to Iraq. I remember thinking how much money it cost the United States, and it just didn't figure. It looked like a job some bombing runs or cruise missiles could have handled if we were really going to go destroy WMDs. I thought we were going after Syria and Iran. When that didn't pan out, I thought psyops, trickery, or some kind of someone was playing us or Bush. At first, I thought maybe Russian KGB or North Korean agents gave money to Iraqi military defectors to give us false information on WMDs to make us look bad in front of the world. But then I remembered how easily the Iraqis were able to manipulate our leaders in the first gulf war. So one Islamic group could very well have deliberately manipulated Bush to weaken us financially by tricking him into wiping out the Baathists at our expense, so another Islamic group could swoop in and pick up the revenue from the oil industry for their holy war.

There are two more big industries that are not above using CIA tactics against the United States, and they too, like the pharmaceutical and food industry, are American industries.

They are US defense contractors and US oil companies! The oil companies during the time of the second gulf war were being watched by everyone. Presidents Bushes close ties with the US oil companies and tied their hands from doing anything to profit from Iraq initially. But the defense contractors needed a good war once in a while for job security. It just so happens that the CIA and defense contractor employees were switching jobs back and forth. It appeared that the companies with ex-CIA employees were awarded the most lucrative contracts. However, the CIA gave President Bush the false WMD report. So who may have manipulated the report? At the same time, there were several high-level Iraqi Military defectors that defected to some of our allies as well us. They also made reports of WMDs. I hope someday to know who was responsible for deceiving the president. I know the CIA who was left holding the bag did not plan the psyop on the president. Well that is not as important as identifying the parts of our country that are under attack right now and how and who is responsible. Since our leaders are under attack constantly, let's take a look at the damage that has been done and how "they" are doing it. They are foreign enemy, organized crime, special interests, big business, and political power hungry groups.

CHAPTER 5

POLITICALLY, OUR COUNTRY has been cut in half by the Democrat and Republican parties. We can't get anything done. We are in gridlock. This is where our enemies want us. So let's look at it. Special interests and foreign enemies have tampered with laws through a fracture in our legislative branch that have our courts filling up prisons with our working class citizens. This is overburdening our public assistance programs with the families of those in prison. In turn raising taxes and causing a riff between the government and the people. Our government leaders that are aware of this are not able to stop it. I talked earlier about how criminals or enemies use all these psychological tactics to bury a problem in litigation. Well if they need help stopping us from fixing a problem. Then they claim to be democrat or republican and every democrat and republican in the county lines up to do battle. So our two political parties are being used to keep our leaders from fixing an expensive problem that is destroying lower and middle class families and imprisoning our working and fighting class men. At the same time, the political parties are used to distract our leaders, so they can be tricked with psychological tactics by our enemies. Our political parties are infiltrated by every enemy, special interest, or thief that is trying to place some of their people in office.

Here is how an enemy intelligence unit would use our political parties in a discreet attack where there can be no trace of their involvement. Say a conservative republican lawmaker is on to a system repair or change that will save billions of dollars and make our system work properly in one of the key areas that was deliberately sabotaged. The Intel unit would find a subject not related to the subject at hand, preferably a special interest movement that the conservative republican has taken a stance against. Then they would find a democrat that was put in office by the special interest group that the republican took a stance against. The reason for the politician put in office by a special interest is that he is focused on what put him in office instead of the good of the nation. Therefore he will be easier to manipulate without chance of getting caught.

The democrat doesn't even have to be a lawmaker. Just a democrat with a special interest agenda. Then trick him into starting a fight with the republican.

Next thing you know, the Democratic Party comes to the aid of the special interest democrat and presto, you have opposition. Plus you spend more US tax dollars to stop us from fixing a problem. The Democratic and Republican party office holders have some criminal infiltration along with the special interest infiltration, and you can bet that clerks, aids, and secretaries' positions are sought out by our enemies also for manipulation, tampering, and sabotage. The political parties which are infiltrated and have separate agendas have also infiltrated our new sources. From these infiltrated news sources biased reports on our leaders are circulated and political attacks are made.

So there is another whole group of people that can be manipulated to attack our government leaders. It is a far more risky way of manipulating a leader as there are investigative reporters like Bill O'Reilly from FOX that will catch false reports and expose the people that produced them. These avenues of using political parties as an invisible weapon are generally reserved for elections and particularly right before the voting. This is because some news agencies have no moral compass and do not care if the responsible side of society sees them report false or manipulative information. That is because those reports are directed toward people that are ignorant in their subject or tactics. The key to the false report is timing when the uneducated and isolated are being targeted for votes. There must not be enough time between the false information being spread and the vote for proponents of the truth to inform the misled population of the truth. These tactics worked magnificently when Obama was reelected. In addition to the news agencies that will intentionally report false information, FOX and CNN were tricked into reporting false jobless numbers by democratic supporters that had access to the reports on unemployment. But let's remember it was in the best interest of our enemies to keep Obama in office. So Al-Qaeda, Hamas, ISIS, North Korea, China, or Russia could have persuaded democratic personnel working on the unemployment report to have altered the numbers to make Obama look good just before the vote on the presidency. So again, we have what looks like a president using Chicago Style political tactics when in fact it could have been enemies of our nation using an infiltration route through the political party fracture. To me, it looks more like foreign intervention than criminal political tactics. The reason I say that is because FOX news was tricked into reporting those numbers.

Everyone knows that FOX news has a republican political agenda with a staff of some of the finest investigative reporters in the world. It stands to reason that FOX is going to find out and retaliate by attacking the president on every issue. This is worse than the standard democrat/republican gridlock as FOX has a worldwide audience. And though the issues brought up are true. Exposing the president's shortcomings to the world weakens our position across the board to both friendly and enemy nations. The amount of scandals that President Obama's administration has been involved in is looking like deliberate sabotage against his administration.

The amount of times the president has been put on the spot has led newscasters as well as republican leaders to show the most disrespect I have ever seen publicly displayed. There is no better way to undermine our country's power than to allow enemies and potential enemies to see that the people of the United States do not respect their leader. That's like giving the green light to ignore our threats and wonder if we can be trusted by our friends. It's too much to believe one president could screw up so many times without the help of our enemies?

Classic CIA style operations are being used by our enemies to get who they want in office instead of America getting the best person for the job in office. FOX and CNN both have a political agenda however they do filter out propaganda issued by foreign enemy, organized crime, and special interest groups. There are a lot of news outlets that print enemy propaganda presenting it as fair and balanced reporting. The truth of the matter is those news outlets have been infiltrated and or manipulated through lies, so they can be used to reach the portion of our population that is ignorant to world events. By reaching the unknowing or ignorant part of our society, they can be tricked into supporting our enemies in their efforts to destroy us.

Our political parties and our news sources are two more huge holes that our enemies are infiltrating the United States through. The amount of chaos developed at this level is easily enough to get average people not to notice all of the attacks and damage that are taking place at the lower levels. The small town, city, and county are just as vulnerable as the higher ups. In fact, they are more vulnerable and are considered soft targets as our small hometown environment does not expect Al-Queda or the likes to be manipulating at that level with the tampering of our laws and American exceptionalism at the workplace in full force. Our prisons were full before anyone even noticed something was wrong! So far, since the prison overflow problem was noticed, it is being attributed to the drug problem. But no one is making the connection from the drug problem to our enemies funding drug cartels to flood our economy which would or should make the cartels an enemy of our nation, therefore supplying harmful drugs would be an act of war. If our nation looked at the drug problem as an act of war, the people that are addicted could then be viewed as casualties of war! That would make addiction a medical issue instead of a prison issue.

But in order to fix a problem like this, everyone in the United States would have to be made aware that we have been infiltrated by enemies that use invisible weapons and tactics and would have this issue buried in litigation so deep they could suck another billion dollars out of us while we tried to fix it. It almost sounds hopeless for the United States to get out of destroying herself. With the confusion, chaos, and system sabotage being instigated by infiltrators from within our system. It looks like we are destroying ourselves when actually we are under full-scale attack by many forces from within our borders. I'm going to go on with my outline of where we are under attack but first, I would like to bring up some differences in culture that is making it so difficult for us to understand our Arab conflicts. Most of the countries in the Persian Gulf area were formed out of nomadic tribesmen called Bedouin. These tribes have fought, killed, raped, and stolen from each other for thousands of years. Their idea of respect and honor are completely different from ours. Respect is forced with the alternative being almost certain death. And honor is stolen. Fathers and sons lie, cheat, and steal from each other. They must become very good at it or face merciless punishment. It is the same between brothers. Betrayal is commonplace and oftentimes ends in an assassination or revenge killing. Their women are treated like stray dogs. The men in the family can kill their wives, daughters, or sister in the name of God for the most ridiculous things.

Women are made to do the manual labor while men think they are above doing any work. Since thievery is a way of life, they look at it like we look at getting paid for a job. So you can compare your coming home with a big overtime check and celebrating to a Bedouin stealing his neighbor's goods and celebrating.

With the discovery of oil came a lot of settling down and building of towns and the mixing of western culture. The wealth from the oil went to very few, and it brought western education and technology to an uncivilized area of the earth that is the most barren, hot, miserable place I've been. It's no wonder they murder each other in the most horrid ways imaginable.

Out of those isolated deserts also came Islamic fanatics with the Muslim religion. The Bedouins raised in isolation and heavily inbred have interpreted the Muslim religion as a callus and ruthless lifestyle that they must live to get to heaven.

The interpretation of the Koran in the isolated extremely harsh environment of the Middle Eastern desert has been as harsh as the environment the nomads live in. That interpretation is that anyone not following their interpretation of the Muslim faith must die. The nomadic tribes were formed into the countries of the Middle East. That is where western culture, education, and technology mixed in with the nomads' culture. So with oil Arab nations grew out of western technology, education, and nomadic tribesmen. That is where the problem lies. Nomadic culture!

Our leaders are not aware that it is honorable to lie, cheat, or steal from us in an Arab environment. Look at Saudi Arabia, on one side they are friends and allies, but behind closed doors they conspire to raise oil prices. Osama Bin Laden is from Saudi. Our ally, Pakistan, hid him from us. When I was in Iraq, the empty wooden ammunition crates lying all over the battlefield were stamped Jordan. Another one of our so-called allies? We should look at the atrocities they commit on their own people. We have heard of Muslim countries attacking their civilian population with military equipment and gas attacks. Here is my view on the first gulf war. One Arab country robbed another Arab country. Then the Arab country that committed the robbery sacrificed its civilian population to setup blocking positions so the leader's army of thieves could escape. I haven't seen anyone describe operation

Desert Storm in that manner yet. The way I came to have that view was having a civilian hospital employee that escaped from Kuwait after the invasion of the Iraqi army to be our guide and interpreter. I was serving with the Second Battalion Fifth Marines when on the second day of the Desert Storm ground war, we were swamped with prisoners. Through our Kuwaiti interpreter, we were able to find out that although our prisoners wore military uniforms, they weren't trained soldiers at all. They were clerks, truck drivers, plumbers, roofers, anyone Saddam's regime could put a uniform on. It was sad and bewildering that anyone could do that to their own people. So where do you think we stand? After hearing stories of how the Iraqi army took infants from incubators and the sick off life support and threw the people in a pile to die and then stole the medical equipment.

We as American soldiers were there to rescue and avenge. No matter if it was American oil business assets that got congress to mobilize us. But we found ourselves in the same place our leaders are still in; that is the land of illusions where all the factions have a smile on their face and a knife in your back. So in a nutshell, some of the Arabs were raised or educated in a western culture, and we can't distinguish the difference between them and their brothers, sons, or fathers that were educated in a nomadic culture. Therefore we can expect all psychological tricks to setup the illusion of trust. If the illusion of trust has already been established, then we must be prepared for betrayal, double crossing, or sabotage. Then we will be robbed in every dubious manor that is possible. Don't worry too much about the jihadists until after we have been thoroughly robbed. The fanatic or radical Muslims that are bred in isolation are a lot fewer than they want us to think. They use all the tricks of illusion with bribery, payroll, and fear to fill the ranks of their jihadist armies. Most of the jihadists are just marauding bandits in it for the plunder. Very few are willing to strap on the suicide vest. You don't see any of the radical Muslim leaders blowing themselves up for their jihad. They are too busy blackmailing the rich Arabs that live around them and looting the towns or countries around them depending on how large of an army they can raise. When they need a martyr for a suicide job they find desperately poor willing to do it for money. They also control the opium which is another way to gather martyrs. However they find them doesn't matter. What matters to them is the illusion that they have these massive armies willing to die in a jihad. When in reality, they are mostly tribal nomadic thieves that are covering up their crimes with religion. I did not mean for my perception of our most immediate threat to cover all Muslims or Arabs. There are large numbers of people who have interpreted the Muslim faith as a peaceful lifestyle and adopted the Muslim ways as peaceful. I mentioned the culture of illusion and theft as I believe very few Americans are aware of much more than the terrorism based on religion going on in the Middle East. Most people are aware of enemy intelligence personnel planning psyops but are not comparing the Arab culture of illusion to a high-tech psyops unit. Well do terrorism is also a psyops!

With that said, we should have a good understanding of our most reckless advisory involved in the not so secret invisible war against the United States. Also be aware that the level of intelligence in human beings is not confined to race, color, gender, ethnicity, or religion. Therefore an Arabic nomad has as much chance of being a genius as the next person. With access to western education, they can absorb knowledge thousands of times faster than an average person. So we should assume the jihad will recruit people at this level that can blend in with the banking and scientific elite of our nation. Now let's get back to the republican and democratic parties being used by our enemies to cause gridlock in solving our nation's problems. There is another group of very powerful organizations and people that use our political system as their personal tool to line their pockets and control the behind the scenes power. Thanks to investigative journalists, the public is aware of the power the Federal Reserve and groups like the Trilateral Commission and the Council on Foreign Regulations has. They don't even have to manipulate or trick leaders. They have the behind closed doors power to make leaders do their will. Now that we have some of our financially elite showing us how the policies of these organizations are being set down by our banks to shift national profit into their own pockets because the owners and staff of these banks are on these committees and groups. We should count these as invisible tactic that are raping the economy of the United States.

CHAPTER 6

JUST IN THE theft and waste I've talked about so far shows how much wealth America had and still produces every year. A lot of the Americans that have used the loopholes in our system are going to have to help us stop the fleecing of American to save it. With the radical Muslim extremist trying to destroy America from within, and the Chinese destroying the value of our currency deliberately while engaging in whole sale theft and espionage against us. We will be hard-pressed to save America. Especially with our system tampered with and infiltrated by so many different groups for so many different reasons. Well, not that many reasons as it is either money, power, or to destroy us.

However the more people that see the massive opportunities to rob the United States, the more of our adversaries will be enticed to jump on us. And with our leadership under attack by foreign enemies, big business, special interests, criminal groups, and terrorists, they are too busy trying to not be tricked or manipulated by the enemies of the United States to even see where the rest of the country is under attack. Well, our leadership is one of the places we have been infiltrated and damaged the worst. Let's look at that a little bit. First, a large majority are put in office to support a special interest instead of a well-rounded leader. Even if the special interest leader is competent for his position, his focus will be distracted for the special interest. CIA tactics like disinformation, character assassination, and other types of smoke and mirrors type tactics are used to trick voters into voting in a less competent leader. Organized crime rigs and bribes some of their people into office. Then there are the rich and famous that buys their way into a leadership spot.

The key to all of these less desirable leaders is money. Even the trickery disinformation and smoke screens hide the truth cost money. So we also have a class issue where a lot of our leaders are from the upper-class (wealthy). Wealth is considered a sign of success and is one of the reasons that some people are voted into office. Here is the problem in that. A financially super successful man can make enough of a fortune to support a very large family for several generations at times. This gives many people the name or affiliation with the success of what was one successful person. What this financial success often does to the family members is puts them at a disadvantage in a competitive environment. What I mean is family money can cover any shortcomings in upbringing education or development. So people from a wealthy family usually won't be as physically or mentally as strong as they would have been if they had to fight harder to get what they have. A lot of them just buy their way through life and if they were stripped off their family's money, it would be a burden on society. And possibly a complete buffoon! But even if they didn't turn out to be ignorant or worthless, they probably were not as good as they could have been as they did not have to try as hard as they would have had to if their financial position depended on it. There are a lot of these types in office. They are the ones that appear to have no common sense. They are also among the easiest to manipulate when these types of leaders are identified. The same money that put them in power will be used to put up the smoke screen to hide the buy-in and setup the illusion that they are qualified.

This financial class division of our population is a subject that starts lots of controversy, so I will shed a little more light on it. Financially successful people that are self-made generally have what it takes to be a good leader. That is where a conflict arises. The average person calls wealthy or financially successful people "rich." Throwing them all into one category. Remember we are talking about leadership in the United States being a fracture in our society in which we are being infiltrated by a diverse group for money, power, and our downfall. Now I'm showing some invisible attacks and damage for a bit that has some effect on our leadership also. That's war of the classes.

It's bull; it would not exist if there were not outside influences instigating a chaotic fight between the rich and the poor which is to put up a smoke screen to cover the fact that the rich and the poor need each other. They work hand in hand. Let me explain. The rich pay the majority of taxes which provide for public assistance, schools, and infrastructure. The poor and middle class is the majority by far of the population that uses the tax dollars. A purpose of the public assistance, schools, and infrastructure is to help the poverty-stricken to climb out of poverty and become a taxpayer and help lower the individual tax burden by not needing assistance and paying a bigger share of the taxes.

Here is where the fight between classes is being started by outside influences. The middle and lower class families are being destroyed by the tampered with laws while the family providers sit in prison. Therefore each family is causing two huge tax bills; one for the cost of the prisons and one for the financial assistance of the destroyed family. Plus this family will most likely quit paying taxes. There is also a probability that this family may never make a financial recovery as the provider will carry a felony status and or a criminal record that prevents employment in many job areas. With the upper-class not aware that this is happening to the lower class, they are saying "Come on, we are paying almost the full tax burden in the US." In return, the lower class and imprisoned are not able to communicate to the rich. Most of these contacts with the affluent are the leaders that got their position from their family's money. So the middle class and below see the bumbling idiots of the upper-class that are being used by outside influences to pilfer whatever is available around their job. The intelligent portion of the middle- and lower class sees the dysfunction. Then hold the financially elite responsible for it. Then we have a conflict where everyone is blaming and categorizing each other. When in reality the laws have been changed and the middle and lower class can't afford to defend themselves in court from the laws. Then the upper-class leadership billets are filled with infiltrators and unqualified wealthy personnel. Then take the two groups of people divided by financial classification and arm the outside interest with all the tools or weapons of psyops or invisible warfare like deception, manipulation, lying, disinformation, illusion, propaganda, persuasion, and what do you have? "Class warfare" in the United States! Just what our enemies and thieves need to keep the middle class and below unaware our laws have been manipulated by other interest and are destroying American families and filling up our prisons. And our leadership is saturated with unqualified rich kids and infiltrators.

By saturated, I suspect over 30 percent, but that is enough to trick the rich and poor into arguing instead of working together. The class warfare trick is important as this is where anarchists from enemy groups will try to get the poor to rise up and destroy the businesses of the financially successful. The financially successful are responsible for a lot of the quote "rich kids" that are in office. Well, let's look at the rest of our leadership. Here is where our strength lies. A self-made millionaire with the initiative and drive takes to make nothing into something big, and successful makes a good leader. A lot of these types have tried to come to the aid of our country. Some have made it into a leadership spot however a lot of them are shot down out of fear by business competitors that don't want their competition in business in a government leadership position. Besides business leaders, we need people strong in science and technology, education, defense, and economics. We have experts in all these fields in some of our leadership positions. As was mentioned earlier, they are unable to get anything done either. As soon as they try our enemies enter through our political parties and all the leaders that are unqualified and special interest personnel line up to oppose anyone that is not from their political party. Our leaders need to weed out the special interest and other infiltrators that cannot evaluate an issue. It should be evident to our leaders by now that they are being manipulated to line up by party to oppose by party. Nowhere are every issue 50 percent right and 50 percent wrong. The spirit of competition and American exceptionalism at the workplace seem to be the culprit as to why no one can see the outside forces at work here.

There is a new issue that is being conjured up in the art of illusion to be used against our leaders. The war on women! Come on, this is beyond the line of ridiculous. It is another invisible attack on our leadership designed to distract. It is also a tactic used to keep women that are noteworthy out of office. Here is my view on women. We love them; we look after them and protect them. In my family, they are highly respected. Beside every noteworthy man is a woman. They chip in and work with the men; they help the men to succeed. If an emergency or attack fell upon our family and a woman was the closet to the problem, she would be the first to help. There are times that a man looks into the eyes of a woman, and he is in love with her to his dying breath. We often look at our daughters as little princesses. Women never had to fight for equal rights in our family during my life. As the earth's civilization evolves, women are evolving from staying at home and raising a family to the workforce and now to helping govern. This move into the workforce and politics in the United States is being aided and assisted by men! From my position with what looks like an invisible attack on American. American women are coming to the aid of their men. Across the board, men are helping women to gain positions in the workforce. Any opposition I have seen from men comes from men that are embarrassed because they could not produce enough money for the family by himself. This movement shows the financial impact that the invisible war on the United States is having. Back to our leadership. This war on women probably came from someone's intelligence operators inside the United States.

Class warfare and the war on women are psychological operations that affect our leadership through distraction. The rest of the psychological tactics like misinformation, lies, manipulation, persuasion, propaganda, etc., are used on voters at voting time and wealth and gender are areas easy to manipulate opposition to a good leader running for office. Foreign intelligence groups working in America count on news reporters to spread false information and to help cause chaos and unrest in the society.

Enemy intelligence personnel are trained to look for any conflict in the society they are working against. From there, they pick sides and insight trouble. Grow the conflict; join both sides of the conflict if that will help expand the problem. This not only drains resources from our nation but it diverts attention from our leaders away from the work they should be doing. The news reporters only need an anonymous tip and if the reporters aren't from reputable outfits like CNN or FOX, the tip can contain propaganda which means that the news is presented to support a specific perspective or agenda. Now we just talked about class warfare and the war on women. I don't believe they even exist. They are made up to divide us so we will be easier to conquer. I haven't mentioned racism yet. There is a conflict that does exist although it should not. Keep in mind that we are still talking about invisible attacks on our leaders. Leaders that have been infiltrated by organized crime, special interests, and bought positions being held by bumbling idiots. Although there are many races living in the United States, I'm going to talk mainly about the past conflicts between black and whites. The relationship between blacks and whites has been strained since the times of slavery. We should remember it was white people that went to war to abolish slavery even though it was black people that were enslaved. That being said, you would think blacks and whites would have a bond of friendship above racial conflict. I've seen racial conflict on the television or in the newspapers, but I was raised in a white Christian home, and we were taught to respect people of all races. We were banned from even using the "N" word since childhood. I'm in my mid 50s now. I stood side-by-side with black men on the battle field prepared to die for each other. We were a band of brothers. So why is racism still showing its ugly little head? Foreign and enemy instigation. All of the invisible psychological and CIA tactics have been used on this conflict since the 1940s. Hitler was one of the first enemies that were discovered to be planning to flood the United States with drugs to destroy our youth. His superior race hype made its way to isolated parts of the United States back then. By the end of the '70s, the first sign that radical Muslims were going to use psychological tactics to insight racial conflict between blacks and whites in America came. It was during the Iranian embassy hostage crisis when the Ayatollah Khomeini released eight black hostages and kept fifty white hostages for over a year. Our prisons were filling up with black people during that era. During this time, the cold war with the Soviet Union was still going. The Russian KGB was using drugs as a weapon against the United States very effectively during this period too. The KGB became heroin dealers in the United States.

The inner city black population was almost decimated.

Again the radical Muslims showed up in our prisons recruiting for Islam and spreading hatred and stirring up violence while white people went after groups like the KKK and other white supremists to destroy them. Black leaders like Martin Luther King stopped the radicalization of blacks. Again blacks and whites should be high-fiving each other. These conflicts of race were put on us by outsiders. The KKK has Hitler written all over it just the same as the Black Panthers have radical Muslim written all over them. We are about fifty years past these outside attempts to destabilize race relations. But still today foreign enemies, special interest, and organized crime are able to put up smoke screens in front of our watchdog groups and stir up some hate in isolated areas.

The reason I say isolated is because areas like that seem to have fewer highly educated people, greater dropout rates in public schools, and less traveled or worldly people. This is where an enemy intelligence operator would choose to start an operation to cause a racial conflict. So they would go to the inner city areas called the Hood or the Ville or maybe rural "West Virginia" or Montana or even Idaho for the all black areas if I were an Arab radical Muslim and they didn't want to leave a trail. They would hire a black radical Muslim from Africa and send him to the Ville to sell guns and drugs and spread hate.

Maybe even try to seduce black men when they are high to kill or rape a white. And they would definitely set the black locals up to get caught by whites. Then you know what comes next? Anonymous phone call to the press. If they are lucky and catch the ear of Jessie Jackson or Al Sharpton who are notorious for stirring up racial conflicts for personal publicity. What do you have? A full-fledged racial conflict.

Enemy psychological operations could be set in motion tricking whites also with hiring a European radical Muslim from Bosnia to start a white supremist militia man isolated spot in the Rocky Mountains or Alaska. From my view, isolation breeds ignorance and ignorance breeds racism. Racism is kept alive in the United States by our enemies and is used as a tool in the invisible war against the United States. Besides distracting our leadership it portrays Americans as racists around the world.

More importantly, it is an invisible wedge being set to divide blacks and whites; just the same as pitting men against women, and rich against poor. Wedges are being driven in between all sectors of our people to divide the power of the people! At the same time, a wedge is being driven in between the people and the government. The government in the US is we the people, for the people, by the people. The division between the people and the government is an "illusion." I'm exposing the parts of the illusion as we speak. So we will talk about that wedge our enemies are driving between the government and the people a little later. The wedges being driven between the people and races of the United States has to involve the Hispanic people. Immigration and work are in the news pertaining to Hispanics. Hispanics predominantly Mexican makes up a large portion of the people of the United States whether they got here legally or not, they are here. The Mexicans, like the Chinese I have met here in the US, are on the average very polite and respectful. However their governments are financially hostile to the United States that leads me to believe these people want to be US citizens, if they are not already. So I view the Mexican people that are here like the Iraqi people that Saddam Hussein's government sacrificed to rob another country. The drug cartels have bought off the Mexican government or most of it. The government officials are looting their own country while their people are poverty-stricken and hungry.

The Mexican government stands by and does nothing while the US government asks for help stopping the migration of Mexican people across the border into the U.S. That constitutes nothing less than a robbery of the US Treasury by the Mexican government. When the people of Mexico arrive in the United States, they go straight to our public assistance offices and apply for emergency assistance. They are provided with food, shelter, medical, and education. They then look for work, prepared to work for less money than the people they are competing for work with because of their desperate financial situation. The US Treasury is then again robbed as most of the money is not taxed and sent back to Mexico. To me, it looks like the radical Muslims partnered up with the Mexican cartels and bought off the Mexican government. Whether the Mexican government just used the US Treasury to support its people or the Muslim extremists suggested that Mexico use its people to deplete our resources doesn't matter. It's an attack on the wealth of the US by foreign interests. It is done sneaky whereas the Mexican people that immigrated to become Americans are made to look like the bad guys when the bad guys are still in Mexico or the Middle East. The drug cartels are charging the Mexican immigrants to bring them over and also using them as mules to carry drugs across the border. The Mexican population in the United States is predominantly workers and their families. There is an element of drug cartel personnel that have setup in the United States and try to blend in with the immigrating workers. They terrorize, blackmail, and murder the Mexican immigrants that are here illegal regularly. They are here only for the money that is available over here. The cartel members are not working. They are selling drugs, organizing gangs, and making the immigrants that are illegal pay their blackmail not to turn them in. The drug cartels are very similar to the radical Muslim groups of the Middle East.

They rob, rape, and murder their own people just like the Arab Muslims. And after they commit crimes against America, they leave their own people standing there holding the bag. This is what it looks like for the immigrants. They get robbed by the cartels that guide them across the border. They are forced to carry drugs on the trip across the border. Once they are in the United States illegally, they get blackmailed by cartel gangs in the US. Then they are made to look like criminal immigrants by the crimes the cartel gangs commit in the United States. Then they are accused of draining our public assistance's money and taking our jobs. Well, I see an invisible strike against the United States by the Mexican cartels and their radical Muslim business partners. They infiltrate and rob the Mexican government then bribe them to let the cartels rob and enslave the Mexican people. The people flee to the United States and the cartel use the fleeing population to hide in while they setup a crippling drug trade. This serves the jihad against the United States by destroying the Americans that get addicted to drugs. Then another large group of American potential defenders are imprisoned for drug use.

Behind the jihad though is the real story! "Money!" The radical Muslims are bandits. The majority wants our wealth, they want to weaken us, and damage us for looks. But the bottom-line is our wealth!

CHAPTER 7

LET'S LOOK AT racism against Mexican Americans. There again is a wedge that is being driven in by our enemies. America is primarily White, Black, and Hispanic. There are three groups that must be split up before war can be waged against us. I see the immigration problem as a theft by unseen enemies using the Mexican people to cause animosity toward Mexican Americans. The unseen enemy intelligence operators then use CIA psyops to spin up racial problems for Hispanics.

The enemy does not want us to get along. Here is my view of Hispanic migrants and Mexican Americans. They are a family orientated people. They are prepared to do the hardest jobs, and they are work-orientated. They are very respectful of women and children and can endure the most extreme weather conditions at work. I worked in the construction field as a company owner and superintendent, though the news carried anti-Hispanic rhetoric because of job losses by Americans. We did not see it in the construction industry. We were glad to have the Hispanic workers whether legal or not. That was because without them, we could not fill out our work crews. By time I left the construction industry, we just could not find entry level workers other than Hispanics. That was a common topic for conversation in the upper echelons of the construction companies. It was generally thought that the computer and technologies boom sucked up the cream of the crop of entry level workers. The overcrowding problem at prisons was not as widely published then as it is now. If you consider the amount of workers that don't work because of a drug addiction. Between the two, that is probably where the majority of the entry level workers really went. Although I just spent a lot of time on people pointing out how we get manipulated into categories to fight about problems that don't exist or have already been solved. I believe the conflicts between the civilian populations in the United States are an invisible attack on our nation, designed to separate the people of the United States to fight each other instead of supporting each other. In addition, these population conflicts are used to distract our leaders from international events, so our enemies can trick our leaders on foreign issues. This means every type of civilian is falling prey to psychological tactics used by criminal and enemy organizations to manipulate us into conflicts. That's rich against poor, men against women, and blacks/whites/Hispanics against each other. That means from the lowest poor person to the highest leaders in our civilian population, we are not aware we are under attack! Now the CIA, NSA, FBI, and military know they are under psychological attack, but no one has noticed that the public is under attack at home. Our enemies have tried fighting our military. Right now, there is no way to defeat our military. So quietly, our enemies snuck past the military. When people talk about war, they think about the conventional weapons. Let me try to draw a picture of what war looks like with invisible weapons in comparison to conventional weapons. Mines and booby traps might be conspiracy and distraction. Machine guns, rifles, and pistols may be seduction, coercion, and chaos. Missiles, bombs, and grenades may be fabrication, lying, and propaganda. Battleships, jet fighters, and tanks could be espionage, illusion, deception. Artillery, submarines, helicopters are manipulation, persuasion, false information. Aircraft carriers, drones, ambushes are misinformation, infiltration, and disinformation.

These psychological warfare methods produce casualties just as well as the conventional weapons do. Compare our prisons to prisoner of war camps, military hospitals to drug rehabilitation hospitals. Military killed in action to civilian graveyards filled with people from drug abuse and related crimes. The military equipment that is destroyed on conventional fighting can be compared to the military equipment we can't afford to produce because our money was attacked and destroyed. Picture the United States homeland as a war zone and instead of bullets, missiles, bombs, planes, and troops crisscrossing in front of you, just picture our nation's problems at home and the psychological tactics crisscrossing and flying through the air and exploding in front of you with stacks of burning money everywhere.

This is what I see as a collection asset. There are two main fractures in our governing system; one at the legislative branch that affects the people and one at the bipartisan party level that affects our leaders. There are infiltrators pouring in both fractures undercover from a hell of a smoke screen setup with psychological tactics I call invisible weapons. These invisible attacks have our leaders blinded, and they can't see the two big fractures that have broken our governing system.

The fractures in our system are causing litigation and gridlock on all issues! Until the fractures are repaired, our country will continue taking damage. With our system damaged, everyone is looting our treasure as fast as they can. Our crooked leaders included. The longer the drain on our wealth goes, the more wedges will be forced in between our population. Chaos, hate, and fear will be stirred into our population by outsiders when they have gotten as much of our wealth as they think they can get. That's when the haters and conquerers will come at us. That's when standard conventional strategies like divide and concur will start showing themselves besides dividing the population up to fight over race and financial class. It will be time to drive in the wedge between the government and the people. This is how good our enemies are! So they think! There is no difference between the government and the people. But the government leaders which are people of the United States will be under so many illusions that they will order military and police "which are people of the US" against rioters "which are people of the US." How good is that if you're an enemy of the US orchestrating this without even having to commit troops to the war yet? It's really easy to convince poverty-stricken masses to attack the leadership. With the rate the US is wasting and losing money, it's not going to be long before we are at this point.

I really didn't want to talk about the illusion that the gout is something you can fight. Our government is "We the People."

People can fight over how they want to govern themselves. But there is no actual government thing or object you can fight. So when someone says the government is against us or is plotting to do things to us that lead me to think an outside force has manipulated that person possibly to do damage or affect more people. Revolution is what our enemies would ultimately desire.

That is how an organized tactician would ideally want the US to act. According to Sun Tzu, a Chinese tactician who wrote *The Art of War* some 2,500 years ago, the best general is the one who can win a war without committing his troops. I don't think one country or person is behind the invisible attacks on America. But I do believe a patient opportunist would jump on us if we financially collapsed and were not unified as one people. I don't want to speculate as to what is coming or might happen. It is the signs of a collapsing society that are showing in the United States that looks like textbook large-scale warfare tactics CIA style. I have covered mostly society's conflicts or problems I can see as a civilian. Plus I have tried to link enemy criminal or special interest to instigating and enflaming our conflicts. I have referred to this as invisible attacks with invisible weapons. I have pointed out what is damaged, how I think it got damaged, and who I suspect did the damage.

Before, I mentioned that our enemies want us to believe our government is not "We the People" and a wedge can be driven between the people and the government. I should have finished exposing damage I believe to be from invisible attacks and weapons on some of our highest government organizations. A lot of reporters are investigating and watching the CIA, FBI, NSA, ATF, DEA, and now the IRS. I'm sure they have the resources to put a finger on who did what better than I can. But I can give a basic view of damage on the surface of these organizations.

The organization with the most visible damage is the IRS. It has been built into an almost uncontrollable monster. And of course this uncontrollable monster is a damaged part of our system. Those invisible attacks with invisible weapons that I'm hoping are becoming less invisible have also been used to deliberately change the IRS tax code to favor or target special interests. The legislative branch was where the infiltration to tamper with the tax codes took place. I suspect the same disinformation tactics, clutter, and chaos were used to distract lawmakers and hide truths while our tax system was tampered with and damaged. Foreign enemies could easily have influenced tax laws through funding discretely the republican or democratic parties. The tax code is now so complex that it takes a small army of accountants and tax attorneys to cost-effectively file our earnings. The power the IRS has gained because of foreign and criminal groups not paying taxes is unmatched by any other collection group or agency in the US. They can seize any personal property, real estate, cash, bonds, stocks, gems, and precious metals, anything short of your birthday and imprison you. The IRS has grown so big and the tax code so complex that people are afraid to file their own taxes as you could owe up to 40 percent of your income if you don't understand the thousands of pages of tax laws. IRS seizures, penalties, taxes, and threats of imprisonment have caused countless bankruptcies, business failures, suicides, and murders. So much so that tax attorneys are trained in mental health to be able to identify potential murder suicide situations. I will guarantee foreign intelligence operators have had their hands in the IRS for a long time. Foreign enemy, business, and special interests tampering have turned the IRS into a terrorist organization that destroys American people and businesses. It has become so powerful and frightening that it was used to stop some republican fund-raising groups during the last presidential election. I'm sure the leadership billets in the IRS have been infiltrated and the IRS will soon, if it hasn't already been used to eliminate bipartisan business competition. The country's leaders have called for simplifying the tax code for many years. Now our enemies and the opportunists are benefiting from a tax system that destroys American business and individual families having used the bipartisan vehicle to cause gridlock every time someone tries to fix this problem. The simplest and most sensible solution has been brought up several times and that is a flat tax. That is so simple and appropriate you would think bipartisan sides would join together, so not even outside or special interests couldn't stop us from fixing the tax code with a flat tax. Well we forgot a very wealthy and powerful group of workers that would be out of work. That would be about two-thirds of the IRS employees, accounting firms, and tax attorneys. They slid into the shadows and used the same invisible tactics our enemies used and buried the flat tax plan in litigation! You can call that the enemy from within or self-preservation. It is the same with the prison system. There are so many people making money off these two categories, there is no way the people will help fix these financial nightmares that are destroying American families and businesses. People think there is endless wealth and if they are profiting from a broken system, it's not their fault. If they don't get the money, someone else will. You can look at the IRS as weapons in the war against America. Americans were manipulated into changing these necessary organizations into tampered with and damaged parts of our system. They are sucking desperately needed tax dollars down the drain and wiping out taxpayers.

Both the IRS and prison system are a double negative gone triple negative as a good percent of the people destroyed by the IRS and prison will be on welfare or some kind of public assistance. Both of these systems have been deliberately made to destroy productive Americans while draining the treasury at the same time. Psychological tactics and infiltration combined over the years have turned the IRS and prison systems into weapons that not only damage the US by daily use, but they can be used by almost anybody to destroy their enemies or competition. This is how an enemy would exploit these two damaged organizations that destroy Americans. Infiltrate American businesses with saboteurs that are going to use the IRS and prisons to get people that are productive leaders. They can submit fraudulent tax reports, promote insider trading, and commit other business related crimes and then expose them. This is a way to destroy smart successful businesses with our system. Business espionage! This used to be used to outsmart your competition. Now it can be used to destroy their competition. All you have to do is report any tax discrepancies or illegal activities discovered by spying on businesses or allege something, and you can tie someone up in litigation that is so expensive you could break a new or expanding company. These sabotaged organizations the IRS and prison systems employ so many people that we are going to have to relocate an entire army of displaced workers to fix these two destructive organizations. This shows a category the US spends money on that is like pouring money and manpower down the drain. If we could pick up the whole IRS and prison system and move that money and manpower to a category that helped the US like Internet fraud and financial defense, we would save trillions of dollars per year. I'll be discussing things like that a bit later. I just needed to cover the invisible attacks that damaged the IRS since they are now up there in size and power with our security agencies that I want to discuss.

The "enemy within." Greed and power is what I'm talking about. Greed and power is what has caused Americans to gravitate toward the CIA, NSA, ATF, and DEA. This puts power hungry American in the mix with foreign spies, organized crime, enemy governments, and terrorist organizations pulling psyops on or around these security organizations. As an enlisted marine working in infantry intelligence to report on these groups is really out of my league. I do have some firsthand knowledge of some behind the scenes. I believe what I learned back in the 80s allows me to pick up on some of the things affecting these groups. I guess I shouldn't leave out the Border Patrol and Customs when talking about our elite security organizations. Back when President Reagan declared the war on drugs that money went to building, several small armies of commandos that seem to have done nothing but waste that money. Our newly equipped black-ops anti-drug commands have made a mess of foreign relations in south and Central America. Americans used to be able to travel without too much concern in those places, but today anti-American sentiment can get you killed or kidnapped in those areas. Our narcotics organizations seem to have adopted the CIA cloak and dagger techniques. This means what we see, hear, and read about our agencies could be an illusion, but maybe not as it appears that investigative reporters now expect these tactics and seem to be not falling for the deceptive stories as much.

CHAPTER 8

WHATEVER THE TRUTH may be, the war on drugs is not working. The war is on the US civilians that got addicted. This is a trick played on the US that took such a long time that nobody has noticed we setup strict drug laws to keep drugs out of the US. Now our drug laws are being used on the Americans that were targeted to become addicts. The DEA and Customs is where I would start if I were an enemy intelligence operator. US intelligence would expect drug cartels to attempt to infiltrate DEA and Customs, but not by enemy governments or organized terrorists. So if I were an enemy government intelligence operator that had drug enforcement, I would suggest surveillance of the drug cartels and organized criminal drug gangs. This would allow the addictive properties of the illegal drugs to spread throughout the US while our drug enforcement agencies sit there and watch. This is exactly what has happened. Whether our agency leaders are infiltrators or have just been manipulated to use these tactics, they are spreading a plague of addiction. This plague is doing catastrophic damage to the US. Just what enemy saboteurs would want? These surveillance tactics have been passed down to the smallest narcotics divisions of law enforcement groups doing "undercover" operations. These drug agencies are mostly private armies. Foreign interference and manipulation plus Americans grab for power has the US wasting billions on drug enforcement. The drug enforcement agencies recruit trained personnel from our military because the drug lords and cartels have their own military defense forces. Why are we building separate little secret drug enforcement armies instead of using our top of the line military? I think it's because our leaders are being manipulated into spending all that extra money because somebody's intelligence group has calculated that it would cost billions to not be able to do the job as well as the US Military could. I was in Panama in the late 80s during Operation Just Cause. President Noriega of Panama was a drug dealer. He was also a drug dealer with a military. Well the US

Military moved through Panama and put Noriega out of business so fast I would think it made people's heads spin.

That seemed like a pretty good way to declare war on drugs to me. Very quick and efficient operation. So why did we have to build all those new small armies from the ground up? It's my belief forces not friendly to the US helped to orchestrate this huge waste. The same smoke screens setup with psychological tactics "invisible weapons" that are used on us over and over again are seen. There is another side to infiltrating the DEA and Customs with agents that are not from the criminal drug organizations. They can use their background in drug enforcement to get into other government positions from different people and or sabotage different organizations. The CIA has been the intelligence or spy agency most people have watched or reported on for the last sixty years. It has been infiltrated by Russian, Chinese, and North Korean spies several times. I imagine there are radical Muslim spies infiltrating their way up the chain as we speak. The CIA teaches infiltration espionage and psychological warfare among other things.

So why don't they use their own students to run the organization? It seems we would have a better chance of not being infiltrated if the CIA leaders were not appointed by the White House! This falls into the wealthy families that put their children in office with money category. Remember, men who build a fortune tend to be the good leaders, and their offspring tend to be less apt to be a good leader as they have been spoiled and pampered and had their problems solved with money instead of the adapt to and or overcome spirit that US Marines live by. A lot of these top spots are filled with people from wealthy or influential families. I know a lot of people are aware of wealthy people buying powerful and important positions in our government.

But I don't think we see the real damage. Most people complain that it's not fair when money influences who gets a position. Or they may see a less qualified or less deserving person get a position. But what they don't see or notice it as a threat. A good percent of those born with a silver spoon in their mouth wind up being naive or gullible. Now you post some people like this at Homeland Security, CIA, DEA, NSA, etc. You have a recipe for disaster. You see these types of terribly rich naive gullible people out in public wearing the most ridiculous clothing. That is how I spot them. They will wear an outfit of clothing you could not get an average person into without kicking and screaming all the way.

People around these financial elites don't tell them they look ridiculous because money gives them so much power. There is a double-edged sword here. We have intellectuals who want the naive types in leadership positions just as much as our enemies do. These intellectuals have an agenda for that person's position and needs someone in it that can be manipulated easily. These agendas generally coincide with a special interest that doesn't have anything to do with what that job is setup to do. I believe special interests and our enemies assist behind the scenes in getting these naive people in charge. Military intelligence teaches psychological warfare the same as the CIA does.

Why don't we teach counter measures to our leaders? Politics are exposing the false information and smear tactics as common methods for tricking voters. Why haven't people been exposing these tactics as being used to control what our leaders do in their decision-making? I believe it's because smoke screens of all types of information both true and false are put in place to cover-up when easily manipulated leaders screw up. And if watchdog groups notice distraction, tactics are put into play long enough to bury bad decisions with clutter. Again, I call these tactics invisible weapons in what I hope is becoming a less invisible war against America. The Pentagon should have exposed these invisible attacks a very long time ago. I guess they don't because they have been used by our leaders on each other as long as I can remember. People copy us all over the world. Some of the best minds on the planet wound up here trying to escape repression and persecution in other parts of the world. We have built a great nation, and in my view, it started decaying about twenty-five years ago. There has been state sponsored theft of patents, copyrights, reverse engineering of our products, spying, and just out and out theft of our products and secrets!

So what would make us think that our psychological warfare tactics would not be stolen and used against us? And look at our enemies. They use military weapons on civilians all the time. I would think that the military and CIA would have expected our enemies' military to attack our civilians. Well I say they have. It's just hard to tell with so many other people using invisible tactics like businesses organized crime, power hungry, Americans in the mix with foreign enemies. I may have started noticing these psyops being used in the US twenty-five years ago, but it has taken all these years to put together how widespread the use of psyops are on the public. Just recently, I have connected the chain of damage that is produced from one trick or psyop or invisible attack whatever you choose to call it. I have fallen prey to the invisible weapons all along that twenty-five years period just like everyone else has. I wish I had written on this topic all along so maybe it would have been fixed by now. Regardless, I hope I am able to make a difference by putting it all in one book. Our CIA has taken a beating in the public eye. The failures of the CIA to provide advance warning to attacks and other major events have them in the hot seat regularly. In the past, I have kind of ignored the CIA's shortcomings because I thought their screw ups were an illusion setup to make them look inept to our enemies. In my mind, this would give them operating flexibility. There is also the fact that their successes have to remain secret to be a success. With technology bringing transparency to intentions and actions around the world in real time, it looks like covert actions are best done with our special operation military people. With all the enemy and special interests, "military contractors, etc.," groups that have infiltrated the CIA, it appears to have become a tool used to waste taxpayer's money. That puts the CIA in the classification of invisible weapons being used to manipulate the judgment of our presidents and their staff. The CIA's psyops espionage and infiltration attempts that have been exposed abroad are also being used to smear the character of Americans. Our people are being portrayed around the world as a population of homosexual criminal war mongering spies that will fabricate elaborate lies to get what they want. This is everything we are not. But as part of bringing America down from within, everything which makes us look repulsive or dangerous is going to be exaggerated and publicized around the world. Do we need a CIA when we have Military Intelligence, Homeland Security, NSA, etc.? With the reputation the CIA has built over the last sixty years, I would think dissolving the CIA would be seen around the world as an upgrade in our nature as human beings and a tremendous savings of tax dollars. Right now, the CIA is very compartmentalized to keep the spies that have infiltrated from learning everything. We are paying for several headquarters groups, several supply, several operations, and etc. No one knows who is doing what. Security seems to have evolved to more of a technical equipment operation. Since 9/11 when President Bush eased restrictions on spying, it seems the CIA has become an internal political spy group to be used on our own government. That's a pretty big waste of money when we have Homeland Security, FBI, and NSAs spying capability. Suppose we are being manipulated by special interests or infiltrators to keep wasting that money? Power hungry political leaders would be interest in keeping the CIA! With their eased restrictions on spying on Americans, this opens a market for information sales in competitive big business. Then there are the enemy government spies collecting information on our capabilities that have spent lifetimes infiltrating. And don't forget our Muslim radical fanatics that just want to financially destroy us, so we collapse from within. As I see it, the CIA has sustained serious damage from invisible attacks, so much so that the CIA could be used as an invisible weapon against the US. For example, with the CIA having the ability to harvest information from American big business, the foreign countries that have infiltrated the CIA for military secrets would be able to gain access to big business secrets that countries like China, North Korea, and Russia would love to profit from. The CIA employs a tremendous amount of people and would require a relocation plan for a lot of them. Seems like it would be easy to weed out the foreigners and relocate the rest of the American CIA employees throughout our other security and intelligence organizations. With our technologically advanced spy equipment, all of our intelligence and security agencies can collect information from around the world. NSA seems to have taken the lead in collection capability by technological sophistication. They too have the same problem of collecting information on Americans. The difference between the CIA and NSA is the NSA hasn't hired thousands of foreign spies that oftentimes turn out to be double agents. To my knowledge, NSA is not running overseas psychological operations or funding private armies or insurrection. They got the same green light as all our security agencies got after the 9/11 attack on spying on Americans. Americans are terrified that their privacy is gone. Along with privacy goes the concern that thieves will steal the information from our government. Big brother is certainly here. We have billion pixel resolutions on photographs from space and microprocessors that can calculate ten trillion complex math problems per second. As I understand,

NSA has received permission to tap our communications companies that use fiber optics to transfer all types of electronic communications. NSA has, according to experts, the ability to clone everything flowing down fiber optics lines so fast that they can keep a copy and the original information still arrives at its destination in real time. The cloned information run through filters that search for key information like names, phone numbers, or words, and separates that information and stores it. Our security agencies have to monitor the US as we have been thoroughly infiltrated. The concerns our citizens have are that stored data can be scanned for any purpose imaginable. With the history of corruption in government, there is good reason for concern. At this point, the electronic transparency that is revealing our secrets, locations, and actions in real time is becoming more of an issue each day. With our system being broken, we are not able to come up with an operating procedure in which we can use the technology for our benefit instead of it being used against us. Though NSA has been around for a while, the tools they are using have just recently been employed say around the turn of the century. That means NSA is under attack by all the invisible tactics that are being used in every other part of our government and society. It won't be long till the NSA's technological advantage is gone. Although our technology is advancing at astronomical rates, the

Chinese, North Koreans, and Russians spend as much money stealing our developments as we spend in research and development. The capabilities we have right now in audio and video surveillance and electronic eavesdropping on communications equipment and computer records needs control measures implemented. The longer this takes, the more damage will be done. And right now, we have the two big fractures in our system that our enemies and criminals are using to stop us from organizing a transparent security system that is for the benefit of "We the People" of the US. I know our public and our leaders are sick and tired of the political gridlock on every issue. It's hard to believe people haven't suspected that enemies of our country are manipulating the democratic and republican parties against each other. It should be obvious that both sides want to stop the decline of the US but each time they meet over how to fix something, they hit gridlock.

If they all just stood back and said, "We are serving our enemies and helping in the decline of America by lining up on republican or democratic sides per issue rather than solving our problems." If we cannot organize the use of NSA by getting past the bipartisan gridlock, that agency will be tampered with changed and manipulated by the power hungry, special interests, enemy governments, and organized criminals that have damaged the rest of our system in the name of greed, power, or destruction.

During the same time, our security and intelligence organizations got the legal go ahead to search Americans for signs of terrorism and Homeland Security was formed. Personally, I thought that was part of Osama Bin Laden's plan to bring us down from within by financial collapse. When I saw the amount of money that was spent on airport security and then a new security agency built from the ground up "Homeland Security," I started thinking that Bin Laden's plan is working. He is manipulating our leaders into throwing money in every direction to stop terrorism. That was when I started giving serious thought to psychological warfare tactics being invisible weapons used on the US. Financially, our airlines were crippled, and our whole airline industry was on the border of financial collapse. I thought for sure Bin Laden planned the financial collapse of the US Airlines Industry. That would have been huge. With all the time and planning that went into the 9/11 attack, I thought after scaring us into spending billions on airport security, Bin Laden's group had come up with one of the stinger anti-aircraft missiles we had given the Afghans to fight the Soviets airpower with. I'm glad I was wrong, but I expected after all that money spent on security, they would shoot down an American airliner for the sake of a good terror plot and possibly cause a financial collapse of the US Airlines Industry. When I started looking around to see what terrorist threats and acts did to the stock market and security spending, I saw it only took a threat to get us to spend money! That is a psyop. Then I started to notice that psyops were being used all over the US by different groups for different reasons. The biggest reason was to get people to spend money! With a little more checking, I found people were being tricked and manipulated by every means possible to spend our government's money, "our tax dollars," in the wrong place. That makes it a waste. Compartmentalization costs money.

CHAPTER 9

LET'S LOOK AT Homeland Security, Border Patrol, and Customs.

You have three separate headquarters with your manpower divided into three separate groups. None of the groups know what the other group is doing. However, the three groups provide security for the US borders. With modern office technology, one department could run all three headquarters. They are all doing the same job, so the administrative needs for each group are similar. In other words, the three groups could be networked together to become more effective operationally while at the same time you could get rid of two-thirds of the leadership hierarchy.

Well again, all the factors that have damaged all of our other agencies are at play here. Homeland Security was created by fear. Terrorism a psyop! Scare us into wasting money. We already had Military Intelligence Army, Navy Air Force, marine, CIA, NSA, FBI, Customs, Border Patrol, DEA, ATF.

Now we have created another expensive agency that is going to help drain our economy, and we won't be able to get rid of it. Remember, we have the bipartisan fracture that any of our enemies can step through when you need to interfere with streamline cost-effective government repairs. The top government agencies I've been talking about have been tampered with damaged and infiltrated. These are the consultants for our government leaders. Is it any wonder our leaders can't figure out what's wrong or what to do about it? Not to mention our system is broken, and the longer we use it in the condition, it's in the more damage we will have to repair. From my view, the problems with our system are like a virus or disease. It has affected our system which used to be productive and relatively cost-effective. Now it's destroying families, wasting our money, imprisoning our population, and demoralizing us. If our system kept at its current level of damaging, our nation could function at this diminishing capacity for quite some time. That is if our foreign enemies didn't attack us while we are in a weakened state. But like another virus or disease, the longer you don't treat it, the worse it gets. So with the fractures in our system wide open and unchecked, infiltration by special interests, organized crime, foreign enemies, and so on will continue. That means every day our system is damaged a little more. And the disinformation, manipulation, and other psychological tactics that are being used to turn the broken system also produce the smoke screen that has kept our nation from seeing the invisible attacks on America. I have been covering the invisible attacks on our leadership and the top government agencies and the damage that has been done through tampering infiltration and out sabotage. The damage being done at the top can probably be seen clearer from the bottom as our leaders know they are under attack with psyops coming from every direction.

They probably know what's wrong with some of the agencies but can't trust their information. Or have experienced gridlock and write it off to bipartisanship instead of enemy or special interest manipulation through bipartisan attack tactics. I think our leaders are too busy trying to protect themselves to be able to step back and take a look at the whole picture as someone like me can. The problem being down at my position is I have no power or influence to be able to talk to our leaders at the top. This is part of that plot I talked about in a class where the upper class can't see what is going on in the middle and lower class because they just don't hang out in the same places. And vice versa. The attacks at the bottom of our society by psychological tactics aren't noticed by the people as much. That is because average people don't expect that they might be attacked with premeditated psychological warfare tactics. These tactics may have been collected, organized, and taught in military organizations, intelligence groups, and espionage environments, but they come from natural human development. For example, when your children try to manipulate their parents to get something as simple as a piece of candy or a cookie. Or when teenage boys and girls tell lies about potential competition to get someone they're interested in to go out with them. Or adults at work that fabricate stories about coworkers to make them look bad when it comes to promotions and raises. I suppose I should talk a little about indoctrination or brainwashing.

When you hear words like these, it makes most of us think about Hitler's Germany or communism in the Soviet Union. Since we saw indoctrination in the past and have studied it. We should know these are tactics used to curb freewill and stop better methods or different methods of doing things. After years of being told the same thing over and over, people just start accepting it without challenge or thought. Next thing you know, it's being taught with no thought of whether it's right or wrong. That's more commonly called brainwashing.

In the middle and lower class, I see brainwashing taking place on a massive scale. The giant food companies that you could call financial elites have successfully indoctrinated the public into eating unhealthy through false advertisement. Our children's health books in school still teach the food triangle of healthy foods. It has milk, flour, and cheese on it still. Bad choices for healthy eating. We're "brainwashed" like cattle being lead to the market for slaughter. Once we are ill due to our diet, the pharmaceutical companies have us indoctrinated into believing that we need their drugs to survive instead of changing our diet! A lot of people are onto the food companies' false advertisements and trickery, but the indoctrination of our police and court personnel is alarming and real. The police that used to serve and protect have almost completely been changed to law enforcement; the indoctrination has been over such a long period of time neither the police nor the public know they have been brainwashed! Look at our courts, the judges, prosecutors, and public defenders are taught "indoctrinated" that not knowing a law is not an excuse for leniency. Our lawmakers are making new laws every day. How could we possibly know the law? You can't even protect yourself with a single attorney any longer. You need a law firm. And in some cases, a group of law firms. It is not only the police and courtroom staff that are being brainwashed. We the people are being brainwashed to go with the police then to court and then to jail or prison. No matter if we are going to lose our job, our house, our vehicle, and our family. The US population is being coaxed into financial ruin and imprisonment. This indoctrination or brainwashing is another type of psychological operation. In the case of law enforcement, the indoctrination in certain areas may be self-imposed for psychological preservation. For example, when police or court personnel are dragging someone's family member away from a screaming and crying devastated family, they have to have something to say to people to justify their action like "it's the law" or now a new one you hear is "impaired driving is against the law." These public servants have to be able to look in the mirror when they get ready for work. So they would have to tell themselves something to justify the amount of families they have to destroy each week. The manipulative enemy and special interest groups play a big part in using indoctrination methods to get us to voluntarily damage ourselves, the enemy within plays a big part in this brainwashing, and that enemy is us! We have begun training the next generation to continue destroying the American family and imprisoning as much of our population as we can get in our crowded facilities. This leads to another breach or fracture in our system. "Education" is how we are indoctrinated. We have seen all over our colleges an influx of teachers infiltrate the school's agenda with their own agenda.

Brainwashing is another psychological tool that I call an invisible weapon. The beliefs and trained responses that are damaging to us as a nation come from being taught them, that's the way it is. American exceptionalism takes over after people hear something repeated so many times; someone will put it into a lesson plan and begin teaching it. Or in some cases, like food companies looking for sales will trick educators into teaching people they need something like milk and cheese! We don't need them; they have some nutritional value, but your body has to work so hard to absorb that nutrition that there are much better sources available. We know better, but we continue to teach it. So the food industry has brainwashed us into teaching it. There are different types of subliminal messages that can be used. Misinformation continually repeated in advertisements is a common method used to implant information in your subconscious. I'll give an example. In one of the milk commercials you hear, "Milk does a body good." Then an education board member attends a board meeting on diet education. The subject of milk comes up and then in the back of that board member's head, he hears that milk commercial saying "milk does the body good," and next thing you know, milk is on the essential food pyramid.

This type of education leaves a trail; it can be covered with clutter and excessive information. But the lecture in the higher education level is used for more sinister agenda than selling milk. For example, radicalism, racism, and political views have all been detected in lectures by teachers with their own agenda. Later in the lives of the students, they could find their support a point of view that was instilled in them intentionally by enemies or special interests. And because that view may have been in the form of lectures, there would be no trial. That means that if their view is one that causes damage, I would call it damage from an invisible attack! The damage being done by our lawmakers has just recently come to noticeable levels across the nation. The education taking place to teach people to continue the damage is starting to surface too. In the court approved substance abuse programs, the people ordered to go must admit to being a criminal to complete the program. If they don't complete the program, they are charged with a new crime. This new programming also teaches that there are no victims being tried in the courtroom. It kind of sounds like the old Soviet Union propaganda indoctrination program! Probably because this education did not come from a government mandate or the department of education.

The enemy from within American greed. There are privately owned companies popping up and competing for contracts to imprison and rehabilitate. The substance abuse programs that are competing for these contracts are the ones coming out with this type of language. I'm not sure whether it's to cater to the court system, or whether the courts are ordering the substance abuse contractors to use this language in their programs. But I do see it as an invisible attack on substance abuse rehabilitation. Substance abuse includes drugs and alcohol. So if our enemies have engaged in trafficking drugs to the US and tampering with our laws, it would be in their best interest to sabotage rehabilitation programs. Programs, doctors, and scientists are developing have nothing to do with indoctrination of unsuccessful information. First, I'll say that addictive materials are being used as weapons by military planners and organized criminals to both profiteer and debilitate personnel at a great financial cost to our country. The problem has become obscene in the scope of financial damage and physical harm to human beings. The leading technological firms are pointing toward neurological science and health through fitness and diet. There are programs like Alcoholics Anonymous and Narcotics Anonymous that have been around for a while. They deal with the psychological and spiritual twelve step programs that have helped many people. But doctors and scientists are looking at things like neuroplasticity which I understand as the map or route your mental communications take and neurotransmitters which carry the information. The mood, chemical balance, and neurotransmitters all seem to lead back to a healthy diet, fresh air, and exercise. There are also mental exercises that experts say stimulate new growth or plasticity to thought paths. This sounds like the direction to rehabilitate Americans that have fallen prey to addiction. I'm a little off the path of the system fracture in the education sector I was talking about. But you should be able to see our education on the drug problem is leading people away from the solution which is allowing mass damage just like our drug enforcement personnel allowing drug distribution rings to operate on the grounds that they are going to catch the big fish when in fact they are allowing addiction to spread. So with indoctrination being so close to education or maybe a way of educating someone without alternatives or knowledge of alternatives that brings up entitlements. What are we as Americans really entitled to? It seems most Americans think everything. Are the enemies of our nation manipulating poor minorities to believe they are entitled to all the benefits we provide through public assistance programs? There seems to be organized efforts to teach the poor how to apply for assistance instead of where to get work to support yourself. I think that comes from that entitlement attitude that has been repeated so many times the poor are becoming indoctrinated. I think this is a tool to keep an army sized force ready to bite the hand that feeds it if you try to take the handouts away that they believe they are entitled to. This is a double-edged sword also. It keeps draining taxpayer's money from the government and keeps the recipients of the handouts unproductive. Entitlements are used as bait for voters as we just recently saw in the Obama reelection. So that leaves the question, what do we do about the poor? Political groups use them as backup votes that can be purchased with government handouts. Our enemies and special interests want to keep them poor to help drain the economy. Big business groups want to keep them close so they can siphon off government money for providing entitlement programs. Organized crime wants them because the poor are less educated on drug addiction and generally have a depressed state of mind that is easy to sell drugs to. So you have businesses taking the money given to the poor off the top. Then you have the criminals running scams and cons and selling drugs to them at the other end of the handout. So after the handout is over, you have business opportunists and organized criminals splitting most of the money. And there stand the poor empty-handed. Then the indoctrination starts against. "We are poor, help us!" It's brainwashing!

The poor don't write to the newspapers. They don't have a public platform to speak from. It's whoever need to exploit or use the poor. The poor are being used as a weapon. Either to rob the taxpayers, help vote into office someone who could not get in on their own merit, or to cause mayhem and chaos to cover another psyop through distraction. Poor is a "state of mind" that is taught. Poor is being created out of people that come from poverty-stricken areas like inner cities that have lost their industry; rural areas with poor crop harvests, changing tides in job needs, drug addiction epidemic, and imprisonment by law enforcement. Group these people together and add their offspring to the groups and you have a sizeable portion of our society. Although public assistance is needed, the way we administer it is the problem. It's an open invitation for theft. And it inspires a lazy nonproductive life. It does not take long to get in the habit of not working. People who are not working are milling about with government money in their hands. This takes away the incentive to even go look for work. Then it draws criminals like flies. So what I see is our entitlement programs encourage criminal conduct and create unproductive Americans. This creates an environment where enemies of our nation can use the invisible tactics to manipulate certain people to teach people they are poor and entitled to everything people who work have. Poor or our lower class though as a group are less educated have just as high of an IQ range as the middle- and upper-class. Through stress, depression, addiction, and alcoholism, the lower class is lulled into a state of mind that old Soviet Style indoctrination will be processed absentmindedly as they are tricked into remaining in the lower class or "poor." Welfare is a trap!

As the welfare program gets bigger and bigger, it has become evident it is not helping people. It appears once someone gets on welfare they're on it for life! It's safe to say that the welfare system is actually an invisible weapon. Once you're on welfare, you become a casualty of the invisible war. As a casualty, you will not become a leader, a provider, or productive member of society. There is a good chance you will become a drug addict and live in a homeless shelter or prison. Your offspring will possibly be inducted into the lower class and indoctrinated by the same forces that tricked you. So the welfare program has been studied by foreign enemy intelligence operators, and they will be pulling strings behind the scenes using all of their deceptive psychological tactics to trick our leaders and voters into supporting welfare. They are fully aware that the welfare system is creating the army they will need to manipulate into their class warfare campaign. Welfare also supports Osama Bin Laden's plan to bring us to our knees from within. The cost of welfare is staggering, and the damage to people and the financial waste is constantly increasing just like the damage from tampering with our laws and supplying drugs to the US. The amount of people on welfare that fall prey to drug addiction has become so noticeable that some states are talking about drug testing for eligibility for welfare. Well if they are addicted already, the drug warfare scored a hit. So if they are giving public assistance, a dirty UA should be a medical emergency. Not denial of assistance or an arrest. Immediate action for a dirty UA with a dangerous drug is detox! I know all people that become a drug addict did not get their addiction from one of our enemies that planned an attack on America and supplied drugs to the US. However, since our enemies are using the drug trade to attack American and drug addictions damage America and cost Americans a lot of money.

CHAPTER 10

I THINK WE SHOULD consider a drug addict a casualty of war. And just like a wounded soldier on the battlefield, apply immediate action to the wound. We would spend less money treating addiction by doctors not jailers. The Arab tenor groups are probably still high-fiving over the new boom in the heroin trade in the US. It coincided with the increased entitlement expenditures. I'll bet a lot of that government money made its way over to the drug lords in Afghanistan.

The huge influx in food stamps. Well a big chunk of those food stamps were traded to drug dealers at half price for heroin. So just like when we send food to the war-torn countries to feed the starving. The war lords or drug lords steal the food. Well in America in the invisible war-torn country, the drug dealers got a good percent of the food stamps. And the drug cartels got a good percent of our welfare class addicted to drugs. I'm writing from up in Alaska where I live on the edge of civilization. The heroin is up here at epidemic levels. Our courts and prisons are already filling up with casualties or addicts whichever you choose to call them. And again, it looks like our leadership is not aware, or does not see all the sides to a planned attack on America.

The courts have not tied the Afghan drug lords and the Muslim jihadists to the problem, or connected the manipulation of our leaders or voters to the tampered laws. I don't believe they see that the poor are targeted as easy marks because of lack of higher education. And I don't think they can see the welfare system as a tool to destroy Americans and rob our treasury. But I did see where there have been meetings on reducing the length of prison sentences for drug charges in Alaska. So Alaska sees the financial burden on the state in the department of corrections. But they don't make the connection to the use of the welfare system as a destructive tool. So there are two treasuries being affected: the feds and the State of Alaska treasury. I hope we connect drugs, poverty, prisons, and laws to our enemies. Every time someone identifies a problem, for example "lengthy prison sentences for addiction," they stop there and fail to connect all the dots, and pin the problem on our enemies and our damaged system.

We are now looking at marijuana legalization! This subject has raised so much interest already; it will be a good subject to watch how special interests and foreign enemies try to affect the damage and money. Money has been the driving factor. Pot legalization will be a great subject to investigate who is behind the scenes manipulating who and what. Pharmaceutical companies will be a main special interest group and the Mexican cartels.

On the other side of the coin, you will have government leaders after the tax income and foreign enemies trying to damage America. Legalized pot is a gray area or uncharted waters so it seems. Well, not to me! Legalized pot is a bad idea! Pot should be decriminalized! I don't see much difference between pot, alcohol, and valium, other than pot seems less dangerous than alcohol or valium. Although I believe pot is less dangerous, it has a lot of undesirable qualities. Pot has been around long enough for long-term research results to be conclusive in most aspects. I'll get into the health factors in a bit, but for now, I'm going to cover the damage pot is doing to our nation legally. Somehow, it fell into the same category as heroin in the Department of Justice. I wasn't alive then to see how that happened, so I would like to speculate a little. Pharmaceutical companies are the biggest drug dealers in the world. They buy off politicians and manipulate those they can't buy through disinformation and smoke screens, "invisible warfare tactics." It would have been in their best interest to manipulate the Department of Justice to make marijuana illegal. Pot is a good sedative and would compete with the pills the pharmaceutical companies sell for relaxation. It's just as possible that a naive lack of knowledge was responsible. Regardless of who was responsible, the prosecution of pot users was costing the taxpayers billions of dollars a year. It has just recently been noticed how many Americans were rotting away in prisons and jails around the country. Just the burden of the law enforcement, judicial and prisons is what caught the attention of the public. Well behind the scenes that left the door open for foreign suppliers to take billions of dollars out of the US each year.

We'll leave it to American exceptionalism. US farmers grew better pot and stopped the flow of billions of US dollars from disappearing every year from our economy. But billions were wasted prosecuting the pot industry. In addition, you have the same burden on public assistance because of broken families. And of course the brutal thuggery of real criminals, "not law breakers," the ones that robbed, beat up, shot, and stabbed pot users and growers because they could not call the police for help. So that brings us up-to-date on the history of pot in the US. Let's take a look at the medical and scientific side of today's knowledge on pot. Smoking pot does the same damage as cigarette smoking on the lungs. Pot seems to do less damage on the brain than alcohol does plus alcohol destroys the liver. So if you consume pot without smoking it, you probably won't need surgery like you would from years of alcohol abuse. In my opinion, pot is safer than alcohol or valium. Here's the downside though. It reduces ambition and goals fade away. THC which is the drug in pot attaches itself to fat cells. Our brain cells are covered in fat. This can block the receptors that catch the neurotransmitters carrying messages from brain cell to brain cell. This causes two types of memory loss, one is complete but temporary. We all have experienced that type; that's when you forget what you're saying in the middle of a sentence but then remember right away. Then there is reduced clarity, and that is permanent. You can compare that to drinking too much or very distant memories. It's where your memory just isn't crystal clear like periods of complete sobriety. My take from that is pot should not be used before all education including higher education is complete. Anyone who has a progressive career or a job where you have to make quick decisions should not use marijuana. If pot was legal everywhere, and I was your doctor, that is how I would explain it.

That's why I would not legalize it. If there was a way to decriminalize it and regulate when and who should use it. That would be the best way to handle the pot issue with what information is available to my knowledge. With Washington State and Colorado legalizing pot, there will be numbers available as to how much financial damage to those states slows down. What I mean is fifty to seventy thousand dollars per year is what it costs to house a prisoner. Plus law enforcement and court costs. Both states are reporting huge tax revenues in the first year. If you add the cost of not prosecuting and jailing pot users to the revenue brought in on taxes. Then add in the savings in public assistance for the families that get their breadwinners back. Then add their income tax from working. Those states will make a financial turnaround. There are some problems though. Some lawmakers are already trying to find ways to arrest pot smokers! I would look at the people looking for new ways to bust pot smokers and see if we see any Muslim support. Look for cartel money. Then there are the special interests making money off prisons and welfare families. Another problem is if Colorado and Washington have too much financial success from legalizing pot, they may not notice that the DWI laws on the Breathalyzer need to be revised as do many of the other laws that are filling our prisons with lawbreakers instead of criminals. I think that pot showing up on our college campuses will show up in reduced American world leaders and technology production. Legalizing pot was simply revising a law. That is the problem that should be noticed; that we need to revise the laws filling our prisons, destroying our families, and sending the US into financial ruin. The pot laws could be revised by decriminalization instead of legalizing which in my opinion was a desperate grab for the tax revenue. The tax revenue created by the pot industry will also be a target for our enemies that have infiltrated our government or can influence the leaders. So I'll be watching for groups trying to isolate the revenue from state excise tax and federal business and income tax. Don't forget we have the enemy within. Organized crime will not be happy with tax revenue being gained on an area in business that they had laid claim to. I would expect to see attempts by anti-American enemies within to get our leaders to organize some new programs to waste the new revenue instead of putting it to help the economy recover. Though I think legalization of pot was the wrong move, I believe the states that made it can salvage the mistake with a public information campaign. The adult pot smokers have children they have high hope for. I've seen adults compare memory game results from when they are high and when they are not. There is no comparison.

It would be easy to get some comparison groups of pot smokers and nonsmokers to compete on grades for the same course. Make the public aware of the facts. If you are in your forties and you dropped out of school or you wait tables dig ditches and your content with menial labor jobs, there is really no reason to put them in jail for pot. But show them what pot does to education possibilities, and you won't have to have a law against pot in school and college. The people will handle it.

Transparency and public awareness is the invisible weapon we need to employ against the psyops tactics that are used against the people of the US by profiteers and enemies. What I mean is with live two-way real-time video conferencing programs like Skype and FaceTime, we can be viewing all members of a group or organization we suspect may be lying or trying to mislead us and transmit audio and video in real-time to a central location that our whole country can view at the same time. Since we are on the subject of legalized pot, I will suggest how I would use transparency and awareness on exposing the behind the scenes. Say the pharmaceutical giants make a grab for the pot industry. They would need the government to "regulate" legalized pot. That means the first place to put cameras and microphones would be lobbyist and lawmakers with close ties to pharmaceutical companies. Then you would look for the legal pot sales and growing companies and post cameras and microphones there to prepare for a smear campaign. Since the smear campaign would probably be on pesticides and fertilizers, I would post cameras and microphones with experts in that field. So the standard invisible attack would be to distract the public from seeing interaction between pharmaceutical companies and politicians and lobbyist by starting an attack campaign or smear attack complete with fear mongering, disinformation, and clutter on the small pot companies while at the same time making pharmaceutical company executives available to be appointed to a government regulatory committee. Then use the fracture in our system at the legislative branch to setup a regulatory commission.

Now if the public was watching all these key areas and sending the information to a central location for viewing, these psyop attacks and forced industry takeovers or robberies using our own system could be stopped. Hypothetically, the pharmaceutical company could be predominantly foreign owned. Once they have control of the regulations over the new industry, they could take all the profit and put the small guys out of business through charging fees to test and regulate.

I used pot for this example of an invisible attack against Americans by a special interest group. By using our system to make a law that we do the work and have to give the money to other people that use our legislative branch to legally steal. When it comes to regulatory assignments that is a backdoor that has been used to steal or destroy American business and money many times. So there was a reason I used the new pot industry and pharmaceutical big business. It seemed to me before the surprise from legalized pot came from Washington and Colorado; the pharmaceutical companies were making a play for the pot industry through "medical marijuana." I believe there are some medical uses but not as painkillers and some of the excuses that were being used.

All in all, pot is a billion dollar business that would be similar to the alcohol industry as far as it will have negative side effects, and it would be better that we don't promote the use of it. But as Americans who need to learn how to recognize behind the back of the CIA style invisible attack methods, the upcoming issue on marijuana will be one where the invisible war on America will be being fought! We need to get pot users out of our courts, jails, and prisons, and away from education and the technical work field. So what you see and hear about pot over the next few years should reflect decriminalization and public awareness pertaining to impaired intellectual abilities; anything other than that, I would consider incorrect or disinformation. Basically, some type of smoke screen. The people or commercials that say otherwise are where we should look behind the scenes to see who is trying to mislead us.

A related topic to imprisoning Americans is loss of gun privileges or rights. I didn't mention this whole topic earlier because I did not want to fall into being perceived as a conspiracy theorist. I'm trying to explain invisible tactics used in warfare that I believe are being used by many groups to either profiteer or destroy America. Then to point out the damage to our system or our nation in each problem area in America. So no, I don't think the government is trying to take our guns. The government is "we the people, for the people, by the people." Our gun rights are under attack! But it's not by the government our enemies would like us to believe. There are a lot of conspiracy theories pertaining to disarming the US civilian population. I don't think it is a conspiracy. I think it is a desirable side effect that has come from the system being broken and the tampering with the laws by special interests and enemies that have filled our prisons and stripped our citizens of their gun rights due to felony status. In the beginning of the problem of too many laws on the books, the Brady Bill was passed to stop felons from being able to purchase guns. Well back then, a felon was someone who raped, robbed, brutalized, or committed some type of thuggary. Today, you can drink three beers and drive and be charged with a felony DWI. Or get caught with marijuana in some states and get charged with a felony. The list goes on. In the city of Anchorage, Alaska, "the biggest city in Alaska," one in four youths is a felon by age twenty-one. It was a big deal when the Brady Bill was passed. Gun advocates were extremely worried about their gun rights. Well they should have been. Now every time you turn around, something has been added to the Brady Bill without consent or prior knowledge of the public. The biggest deterrent to an invasion of the US has been the fact that America's civilian population was armed. Today, there are tens of millions of Americans that either cannot own or purchase a firearm. That is a pretty big chunk out of civil defense. With the expanded Brady bill, I'm sure we could track that back to special interests that are profiting from our prisons filling up and the ranks of our public assistance overflowing. With the civilian public being swept up and put in prisons on behalf of "law enforcement," it only stands to reason that people used law enforcement will lobby for more and more ways to take away the civilian populations guns. It's hard to figure why our leaders don't know why so many law enforcement people are being shot. It only makes sense when you look at the financial destruction of family after family. Though it makes sense, it's a horrific shame. The enemy and special interests then funnel money into gun control advocacy groups and continue to find ways to disarm Americans. It is a very effective way to disarm American civilians, but it is wrong in every way possible. First, special interests groups tamper with our laws. Then our police evolve from serve and protect to law enforcement. Then starts the imprisonment of the civilian population. Then the public starts resisting and taking revenge on law enforcement. Then lawmakers supported by our enemies and special interests start disarming the public. That would be a great strategy if it were preplanned though our enemies have to bring us down from within because they can't win a fight with our military. I think the disarming of our civilians is a perk our enemy got from special interest groups, funding new laws, and our police becoming law enforcers. Although legalizing pot was probably the wrong move in the long run, hopefully it will point out a relief of burden on the prison system. From my view, three-fourths of our prison population should be released, and the laws that put them there revised. That would untwist a lot of the items that are causing fear, hate, destruction of the American family, and financial decline of our government. Not to mention our civilians will stop shooting law enforcement personnel. If we were able to relieve a burden as damaging as the law enforcement problem, that would give us the presence of mind to fix the fracture at the legislative branch and start eliminating and revising our laws.

CHAPTER II

WHEN THE US goes to war, we use psychological warfare tactics to confuse or trick our enemy. And we use electronic warfare tactics also such as electronic jamming or flooding the airways with false communications and other signals. So I have been talking about an invisible war taking place in America. The tactics and weapons that are being used are secret and invisible. I've talked about a chemical attack, "illegal drugs," and psychological warfare with CIA type tactics. Now I am going to compare Internet hacking and fraud to electronic warfare tactics in the invisible war in America. We are all aware that there is full-scale theft taking place on the Internet. We have our American thieves, but they are insignificant in comparison to the state sponsored theft that is going on against America by foreign governments and organized crime. We are like one big fat juicy money pie, and all our enemies are after it through the Internet. Now foreign thieves and governments do infiltrate our business and government offices for the purpose of theft in addition to other tampering and sabotage. But that takes a lot of planning, time, and money. Plus there is a serious risk factor. That means the majority of the thieves are sitting in another country, safe and sound. There are office buildings in other countries that have hundreds of operators on a keyboard doing nothing other than attacking American companies. Of course every aspect of our government is under attack. I did some research on government grants approximately two to three years ago and found that out of eighty-eight websites, eight-four of them were fraudulent. I checked several times at later dates, and all the fraudulent sites appeared to still be operating. Internet theft is staggering. It is uncomprehending that no organized effort has been made to put an end to it. It is another big fracture in our system that criminals and our enemies are pouring in through, and money is pouring out of.

Here is another major invisible strike in the invisible war against America. Yes, it's obvious we are being robbed, and the methods used change as fast as we discovered them. But I want to expose the whole picture or connect the dots as to how the theft continues year after year. The fracture in our system that has allowed Internet theft to thrive is kept open with the same combination of invisible weapons or "CIA style tactics." The republican and democratic parties are a straight on passage through that fracture in our system to the fracture at the legislative branch. Funnel some money to lobbyist and fire up that invisible weapon, and no reasonable way to stop Internet theft will make its way through the legislative branch. Then our enemies will cover-up any legitimate ways to stop Internet theft with disinformation, clutter, illusion, confusion, and so on. However, individuals and individual companies are fighting this theft individually. This puts our defense capabilities at a disadvantage. They are fighting against organized crime at the government level from hostile governments.

Since I'm calling Internet theft electronic warfare, electronic warfare is an invisible tactic. I know the theft going on is visible, but I believe the other components keeping the door open to theft were invisible to the average American. In addition to all the methods used to steal over on the Internet, these highly organized high-tech thieves and enemies have other tools in their arsenal of invisible weapons. Viruses, worms, and other malware are being used to steal money and information as well as sabotaging those who are attempting to stopped the theft. These software bugs are also being used to extort money from people to let them back in their computer after criminals lock computer owners out of their own files. The malware and viruses are loaded in our computers over the Internet, and the people that loaded them in our equipment then offer to sell as a program to get rid of the problems. There are viruses that are designed to just destroy information. The US government alone is forced to spend billions on cyber security so in a plan to take us down from within by financial collapse. That makes sense in a big way. Just like attacking with our airliners on 9/11, we spent billions again on airport security. Besides the anarchists like the radical Muslims, most of our enemies are after money or technology. State sponsored Internet crime or "Electronic Warfare" is out of control in China. Their government is run by criminals; they have been caught in every kind of fraud, theft, counterfeiting, and criminal state sponsored crime against the US you can imagine. They also ignore all patents and copyrights to anything US owned. In other words, if we record a CD or publish a book, they will just copy it and start selling their own copies. The trade talks that started before President Obama came into office were to address that problem. I haven't seen that the talks slowed the Chinese down any on stealing. I think some of the cheap copies or fakes of our own products have been stopped from being sold back to us but not in other places.

The wholesale theft by the Chinese government against the US is catastrophic. I don't know what the level of theft in US military secrets and technology has netted the Chinese in gains. But I believe China is playing chess with the world, and in the last twenty-five years has gone from a position where the US could have checkmated them in one move. To a position, they can become a formidable adversary. And they have done it primarily from stealing from the US. Recently in the news, a Chinese Internet company named Alibaba became the richest Internet giant by copying Amazon.com. The Chinese company now has alarmed the banking world as they are now two-and-a-half times the size of Amazon and have records of hundreds of millions of credit card numbers. It is feared that the Chinese government would have access to stealing. Well fear not, if that information is traveling via the most secure route of fiber optics through any of the communication hubs in China, it has been captured by the Chinese government As well as our NSA most likely. That is because the private companies that sell the components to clone that info and send it on in real-time sell to more people than just the NSA. So as far as that goes, any communications that an American makes from the Asian part of the world that travels on

Chinese owned communications companies can be grabbed. The question is how well these private companies over there encrypt sensitive information. And have the Chinese stolen our abilities to decode encrypted information? It's a shame the criminal Chinese government has such a death grip on their people. They would make a good ally in the war on terrorism. For now though, the Chinese government is probably one of Al-Qaeda's best allies in the war on our check book. Hackers are working around the clock on every one of our system and infrastructure categories from air traffic control to hydroelectric dams to pentagon and military. The banks, schools, businesses, communication companies, and science and technologies are all being probed or broken into daily though the criminal and opportunist leave a trail that they have broken into companies by stealing and revealing secrets or money.

I'm sure the organized military cyber sections are compiling ways of getting into our computer systems and keeping them secret. They would be very valuable to use at a key specific time in conjunction with an attack on America. An attack of disinformation and clutter across our computer and communications networks would be another electronic warfare tactic utilizing psychological tactics with electronic warfare tactics. In the electronic theft of money lies another crime–the illegal electronic creation of money by big banking. Or maybe it isn't even illegal as the leaders in big banking know where the fractures are in our system. So you can bet the bankers went through the legislative branch and paved the way. As a matter of fact, I believe they call it the "Fractional Reserve System." That is the way the Federal Reserve prints up money that we don't have. And of course this money is sold as interest bearing debt. Insider trading or theft is the closest thing that I can compare that type of banking to.

I'd like to see the planning and manipulation, bribes, and murders it took for the banking or financial elites to set that automated siphon of Americans' tax dollars up. The trickery the financial elite use to rob us is truly invisible weapons; they are able to trick our smartest financial advisors or out maneuver them through preplanned legislation. I think great care was taken in making the financial system way too complicated for most of us to be able to watch for fraud scams and theft. Between companies like CNN and FOX, they could put a good presentation together as to who did what and who tricked who into letting foreign financial elites herd up the American middle class like cattle and siphon off their money! However, until transparency becomes crystal clear and wide spread, companies like FOX and CNN can still be forced not to air a story that can trace conspiracy through our banking system and place responsibility on individuals!

These financial elites are said to have more financial control than most any countries on earth have. So even if say FOX news reporters like Neil Cavetto and Bill O'Reilly went rouge and investigated say the Federal Reserve System for the public. The financial elites could order the government officials that are on their payroll or own their debt to block all investigators and sight security issues as the reason. Even if the reporters were able to secretly get the information, they'd have to organize a coup of their news network to air the information, and then watch as the financial elites destroyed their company and probably came after them individually. That's where widespread crystal clear transparency can be used. When average citizens can simultaneously view files, witnesses, and events with two-way real-time audio and video, the criminals won't know who exposed them as everyone will be watching or exposing their activities. The Internet, although being the access point for criminals and foreign enemies, can be our salvation by turning the lights on who is doing what. Cyber warfare and big brother are here. As I write this information, one of the biggest and most important battles in invisible warfare in the US is coming up.

The control of technologically advanced audio, video, and communications equipment and the internet. We the people of the US are about to get left out of having any control of the internet and equipment and in return, we will be monitored and controlled with this technology. We will become debt slaves as a nation until we collapse from within. The Internet is already being used as an invisible weapon against us for theft and sabotage. I don't want to speculate like I just did. So let's go back to the Internet being used to commit catastrophic theft against the US. It has become public knowledge as to what has been done to us through the Internet. Potential power and financial gain and control can be taken by influencing legislation to give control to a small group of individuals. If a small group makes the new laws for the Internet, we stand to lose, watchdog, and whistle-blowers along with unbiased news on public media sites and private websites. There are several special interest groups that would like to be able to control the news we get. The major carriers can be controlled by the big money special interests as they own the companies that pay to advertise on the news channels. So if they can't control public media and private blogs on the Internet that takes their control of the national news coverage away. It would do them no good to threaten to pull millions of dollars in advertising from FOX or CNN not to run a story that will harm their profit margin when it would be all over the Internet. There are other foreign and enemy interests that have infiltrated US government positions that would help big money interests push through legislation to censor internet media.

Video surveillance and law enforcement groups are already preparing to take control of the rights to use our cameras where and when we want. If we don't get together on repairing the lawmaking process, our enemies and special interest groups will legislate control of our technological wonders over to them. Then we will be paying foreigners to use our technology and having our enemies and criminals using the technology against us. So far, fraud and clutter have people confused as to what capabilities we have that people have not figured out. I'll explain. I have what I consider high-tech audio video real-time two-way security. And I don't pay Brinks or any other security company. I started with a free download of Skype on my desktop with a webcam. Then I programmed Skype to automatically answer any video calls, and I could leave home and check inside my house from other computers. Well that has evolved into four Apple 5S smartphones with telephoto lenses for the cameras and Wi-Fi plus a laptop with a webcam and Wi-Fi. I have Skype on all the devices and software to monitor six video calls at a time on my laptop and desktop. So essentially, I have a portable and mobile two-way telephoto camera security system that I can monitor all the cameras at the same time while driving down the road with my laptop with me or sitting at home. Now this is just a hobby. I don't have any need for a security system, so I don't worry about counter measures like encryption or cyber-attacks. The point is it's free with my phone and internet services. My Apple iPhone 5S are multilingual, so you can speak to them in different language and the phone will translate it. My next investment will be attaching a webcam to a telescope to add some long-distance capability with future plans of subscribing to a satellite company that has optical capabilities.

I had envisioned other community members outfitting with similar equipment and setting up a civilian volunteer network linking home security to emergency services on a live real-time two-way video security network where a headquarters monitors a community video security blanket.

With a system like this, a surgeon and EMT could direct the first on the scene before emergency help gets there. With long-distance cameras and mobile cameras, criminals would have a hard time getting away. Gang and stalking activity could be easily spotted. It seems opportunists and profiteers will commercialize the free security and sell it back to us or legislate us out of it. The forces that want to destroy the US will be supporting the company that just sold the New York Police Department a similar system, except it doesn't include civilians being able to use it. It was sold to the police for law enforcement! Not public safety, enhanced security, or cost-effective community operations! But to sweep more civilians into the prison system at a faster rate. It seems like we better organize a counterattack against the invisible war on America. So far, the problem areas that are under attack that I'm reporting seems to make this report look like the state of the union behind the scenes. I have spent so much time watching while this catastrophe unfolded over the last twenty-five years. I am embarrassed that I kept thinking someone would stop the downward spiral of the US. We are made to look like fools while special interest, profiteers, and criminals rape, pillage, and plunder our country right in front of our population as our bloodthirsty enemy watch and assist in our financial destruction. I am not educated at the level that our leaders are, but let me present a simple view of how I would fix the American system. KIS is an acronym used in the military. It stands for "keep it simple." So I am going to recommend a plan to get the US out of debt, increase our ability to defend the US within our boarders, and restore our stature as a world leader. And I am going to lay it out at an eighth-grade level. That is why I mentioned KIS. I want everyone from the bottom to the top to understand the recovery plan. I will refer to it as the counterattack in the invisible war against America. I am not in a government leadership position, but I am trying to get the attention of our leaders as well as the people of our nation. If I was the president, I would want to inspire every man, woman, and child in our nation to chip in and be part of a national movement for all of us to work on the US recovery plan. I would want to counterattack with every man, woman, and child we have!

CHAPTER 12

EVERYONE NEEDS TO be a soldier in the invisible war against America. Our money, credibility, and character are under attack.

Here is a list of the invisible weapons that are being used! Disinformation, persuasion, manipulation, chaos, clutter, coercion, seduction, disarray, confusion, exploitation, false information, illusion, lying, façade misinformation, deception, propaganda, fabricate, conspiracy, and distraction! And here is a list of some of the larger groups that are attacking with these weapons called psyops: North Koreans, drug cartels, Iran, the pharmaceutical industry, drug lords, big food corporations, China, Syria, oil industry, defense contractors ISIS, Al-Qaeda, insurance industry, radical Muslims, organized crime, Russia, bipartisan politician, big banking, foreign high-tech criminals, and all of our special interest groups! This is a worldwide invasion army that has descended upon our system and our money.

The system has been damaged, and our money is being wasted and stolen at an astronomical rate. We are at risk of being destroyed from within! This is why we need every man, woman, and child. The US cannot have their leaders go behind closed doors where all those psyops can be used on them to make a recovery plan. So the legislative branch is where I would start. That is the loophole in our system that our enemies, big money, and special interests poured in through. They rode in on the backs of lobbyist and changed and made so many laws it broke our system. All these groups have built a defensive perimeter of psychological tactics or "invisible weapons" around the lobbyist and lawmakers.

So we need to form an army to help the lawmakers reduce our laws to simplest form and throw out the excess! Well, if we fix the nation, we will have some displace workers. One of those groups of displaced workers will be lawyers, and that is a powerful group. So we will have to have meaningful work for them to transfer them to, or they will block us from trying to fix the broken part of the system. The lawmaking corridor! If we abolished laws making substance abuse criminal, we could cut the workload in our courts in half. That would free up lawyers and related professionals to form the army we would need to fix our laws. This would give the most important groups of highly educated Americans a purpose and a worthy cause. This would initiate 50 percent of the prison and jail population to be sent home. In turn, this would save massive federal and state tax dollars. So what we will essentially be doing to fix the system is shifting key workforce personnel out of jobs that have a negative financial impact on America to an area that benefits, strengthens, or saves money for the nation as a whole. You can compare it to a military commander shifting his units to areas where they will have the most effect. This would be the first step in our counterattack on the invisible war on America. So in step one, I would shut down or abolish lobbyist. Then order the legislative branch of the government to rewrite or dispose of all laws on the books to reflect a streamline cost-effective set of laws to protect America and the people of our nation. If this got done to the best of our ability, the future great minds of lawyers could be devoted to something productive in society instead of arguing in a courtroom over a set of laws that are obsolete twisted, don't pertain to, or are mixed in with tens of thousands of other laws.

We will need another step in our counterattack on America's invisible war. We will need to form criminal psychological warfare police. Psyops/CIA tactics are how all this financial and productivity damage is being accomplished and covered up. I'm going to list the steps or places that we are going to counterattack in a moment. I wanted to bring out the two main problems I felt that caused the decline of the US as all the other contributing factors relate back to these two main problems. That is years of our enemies and special interests influencing what laws were made which has broken the system, and the psyops that are used to manipulate and cover-up the broken system. The two steps I have mentioned, if you will notice, intertwine and affect the other steps. That means they are all connected, and there is no specific order in which I think they need to be listed. In fact, all the steps should be carried out simultaneously or as close to it as possible to get the full and noticeable effect of change in the most expeditious manner possible. However, none of the steps I'm about to cover would work without fixing the first two steps as these are why nothing our country has tried has worked over the last twenty-five years. In addition to that, the US leaders put all our money in one plan each time instead of spreading their efforts out in a multifaceted plan where each component helps or relieves a burden on another component of the plan.

Since the US is broke, we should try to fund all system repairs with funds allocated to pay trained experts in fields deemed as an incorrect expense, or an expense that has been forced on us by those who have manipulated our laws. For example, moving lawyers out of the court room to the legislative branch; move a portion of IRS employees to Internet security; moving prison population to infrastructure repair; move prison and jail workforce to medical field for drug rehabilitation of civilian population; move law enforcement units back into crime prevention position; mobilize welfare recipients to support position shifts of workforces changing jobs; move portion of military conventional forces to border patrol. These transfers of the workforce to the areas they should be working will save hundreds of billions of dollars each year in not arresting and imprisoning millions of Americans, stopping Internet theft, and stopping big banking and big business fraud and theft. Stop in financial conspiracies protected by laws that thieves manipulated into place. Basically, we would displace large groups of educated workers doing jobs we should not have to do if our system hadn't been tampered with. They would be doing jobs that would be saving the US billions in system damage and theft. Providing productivity and security while putting the wiped out portion of our society back to work and creating taxpayers!

I have spent many years thinking about what I would have done when I see our leaders put together plans designed to benefit Americans or resolve a problem. And every time the plan is so complicated that only a handful of people can understand it and its obvious greed is going to suck the cream of the cash off the top and preselected contractors get the rest and the people stand there holding the bag. I have also seen a lot of plans proposed that I thought would work but got shot down with invisible weapons "CIA tactics!" So I have kept the thought of keep it simple (KIS) in my mind and came up with a recovery plan that I think eighth-graders and up can understand. It is a nine-part plan, and it is comprised of bits and pieces of other plans or peoples thoughts that were either shot down without being tried or tried by themselves to no avail. The plan is made to stop what I say is an invisible war in America. I would call this the battle plan for the counterattack against those forces attacking our system and stealing our money. So leaders and interested parties look for parts of the simpleminded thoughts that come from this soldier's honest concern and see if my unqualified effort to help could be converted into a format using the proper terminology to be used by our congress to reverse the decline of America.

CHAPTER 13

Nine-Part Recovery Plan (Counterattack)

1. **Abolish Lobbyists.** Organize, simplify, and reduce the number of laws–reform two-party politics.
2. **Simplify tax code** by implementing a flat tax system–forgive noncriminal American back tax debt.
3. **Reorganize crime prevention** to include psychological crime units and civilian cybercrime units. Change units with primary mission of law enforcement to a mission to serve and protect the civilian population.
4. **Declare drug addiction a noncriminal medical illness injury**. Develop amnesty and pardon programs to

encourage recover. Convert excess prison and jail facilities into drug rehabilitation hospitals

5. **Require entitlement programs and welfare recipients to work** at least a part-time job, volunteer work, or participate in school or some other form of education to qualify for benefits.

6. **American human relations awareness.** Advertisement and education to make Americans aware that our enemies and special interest groups that have an interest in causing conflict in the American population through race, gender, IQ, sexuality, age, financial class, religion, etc.

7. **Cutback foreign spending.** Redeploy overseas military assets to assist US border patrol in stopping illegal immigration and drugs from crossing the border.

8. **Reform Banking.** Organize Federal Reserve System and US Treasury to profit the United States of America only. Phase out fractional banking system. Pay off interest bearing debt against America.

9. **Modernize health, education, and infrastructure.** Investigate education by category to find material used to

teach our teachers to teach us to follow the laws that are destroying America.

This nine-part plan is a rough draft laid out as simply as I can. I realize most of our leaders could only say we can't or have already tried to make some of these changes.

CHAPTER 14

WELL THE US Marine Corp is renowned around the world as the best fighting force in the world. Here is my take on that. The word *can't* do not exist in the vocabulary of a marine. It has been replaced with "adapt to and or overcome." That is what we the people of the US need to adopt. I am fully aware that I do not have the education or knowledge to have suggested the best options for parts of this plan. The object of presenting a plan from a middle class mentality was to reach the majority of our nation. Financial class has nothing to do with the level of intelligence of a person. So I am hoping to get the attention of those people who do have the knowledge and education to fix the different parts of our system. And get the attention of the masses to ask them to have our leaders evaluate plan eighth-graders can understand, and our leaders could make work. I would like to bring the people of our nation and our government leaders together to look at what I think I see! An invisible war taking place in and against America. I would like to unite the people and the government to work on a recovery plan everyone can participate in. Transparency along with an easy to understand plan that includes millions of Americans working on it and millions supporting it and millions watching our backs.

This seems like a formula that could work. I think public debates could be held to identify the positive and negative side of a proposed plan before we tried to implement it. The one part of my plan that I feel so important is waking people up to the psychological manipulation that is used across the nation at every level down to the individual household. Our whole nation accepts psychological tactics as the main method that is used against us to confuse, trick, and manipulate us and also to hide the truth in smoke screens of clutter and distraction. We would have millions watching out for these tactics which would make them hard to use from here on out. With our whole nation watching for psyops, I believe our leaders could field a plan that had not been manipulated by our enemies, special interest, or big money! The nine-part plan I proposed is all connected. In other words, what is proposed in one part play a part or affects the eight other parts of the plan. So I am going to explain how I think each part of the plan that is successful enhances the possibility of success for the other eight (8) parts of the plan and how it all fits together.

Keep it simple and transparent, recruit the public to help. In part one, I suggest to abolish lobbyist reform two-party politics and simplify our laws by reducing them to simplest form, getting rid of outdated and inefficient laws then organize our laws. There would have to be a priority for the law changes that are needed in the other eight categories. For example, pass legislation to declare drug addiction a noncriminal medical illness injury. This would put into motion so much new work and saved money that could start immediately with probably the simplest legislation needed to get any part of the plan moving. If I was the president, I would justify this move on the grounds that our enemies that are foreign governments, Muslim jihadists, and drug cartels planned against our civilian population for the purpose of taking their money out of our economy and or disabling as many Americans as possible with addictions, also causing a tremendous burden on the US financially in caring for those who get addicted.

If we truly declared war on drugs, that should put addicts in the category of casualty of war! Outsiders deliberately put this invisible strike on us. And it hit us hard right in the pocketbook as well as disabling a large portion of our fighting force. Let's not forget the damage to productivity in the labor force and science and technologies etc. This one problem alone affects us in so many directions that it is difficult to add up the damage. I look at our enemies using drugs to damage us as a chemical attack just like using mustard gas or nerve agents. When you release the chemical agents into the air, everyone who walks past them becomes a casualty. It is similar with illegal drugs except when a shipment is dropped off in the US, it begins to spread through distribution and almost every hand it touches becomes a slave to addiction. The enemy leaders and drug cartel leaders know that this is how it works. So they know it is a sure thing when it comes to taking money from our economy to disabling the people who become addicted. The drug cost so much money that it's only a matter of time before the drug addiction drains every bit of financial resources the addict has available. The drugs also take a tremendous toll on the human body. It normally doesn't take that long before an addict is not able to make it to work any longer. This opens up some additional costs. As the addiction progresses, productivity at work goes down so the employer takes a loss in profits. The addict attracts violent crime as criminal can now rape, rob, and pillage the addict who cannot call authorities for help as he or she is not considered a criminal instead of a casualty of the invisible war against America. But don't worry; the addict will eventually become a real criminal. The average addict will be reduced to becoming a thief, robber, burglar, prostitute, con man, or some type of criminal to support the addiction. And the hierarchy of the drug cartels and their supporters know all this in advance. The funny thing or not so funny thing is that we as Americans know this by now ourselves. And yet we let our narcotics police setup surveillance on drug sales to try to catch the guys who are not even in our country. What an oxymoron. That makes about as much sense as charging across open ground at machine gun positions did during trench warfare days. Here is what we have to remember. Our police were tricked into surveillance tactics by our enemies. Lies, disinformation, persuasion, infiltration, and sabotage were all used. Now with one law changed, we can make this start going away. Remember all the other parts, this plan will affect the repair of the multidirectional damage that ripples off this one type of attack against us. Transporting drugs into the US should be an act of war. The damage can be stopped. In part seven of the plan, we would deploy our military along the southern border to help stop the flow of drugs into the US. In part four, we would be converting excess jail and prison space into drug rehabilitation hospitals.

Alcohol is also a drug; the addictive properties of alcohol have been known for ages. Given this knowledge was known by lawmakers, special interest, and foreign enemies; it is obvious how we got manipulated into having alcohol legal then putting people in prison for using it.

The premise used was drunk driving. CIA tactics were used to trick lawmakers that were pressured by lobbyists that were hired by special interests to change our laws. By giving legal relief for addiction, this could clear out 50 percent or more of our prison and jail space. The addicts that should be released are the ones that broke laws by possession or use of drugs or violations of drug related laws. It's unfortunate for those addicts that turned to crime before they were imprisoned as they may have committed some type of heinous crime. Justice for these people would require appropriate punishment for the crimes that have victims other than themselves. There is some culpability involved with the system as the tactic of watching a drug house to try to locate suppliers allowed the drug addictions to spread. Then over time, let the addictions turn the addicts to crime to support the addiction. That being said would leave a little room to get more people out of prison or reduced sentences. Let me explain what this clearing our prisons of Americans that became addicted to some type of drug will do for America. Besides saving billions of dollars, it will give that portion of our population hope. To be labeled a criminal and have your life destroyed then get imprisoned is psychologically debilitating. This is where terrorist organizations are recruiting. This is a very disgruntled group of people. It is not just the addicts, but the people who love the addicts, wives, husbands, brothers, sisters, children, fathers, grandparents, friends, coworkers. Addicts started out as very good people and most of them would never consider committing a crime.

This is also the group that is taking revenge against law enforcement. These families of the addicts are desperately trying to save a family member or friend when the system takes their loved ones away from them. The radical Muslims are recruiting full-on in our prisons. In that environment of isolation and anger, hate and despair, Americans are tricked into becoming homegrown terrorists in prison where it is very easy to use psyops to channel those emotions against America. That was painfully clear recently in Moore, Oklahoma where a man was recruited by radical Muslims in prison. Then shortly after his release, he cut the head off a coworker. These sick psychotic terrorist tactics are being developed in the areas of the world that these drugs come from. The Oklahoma case is evidence that drug use can twist your mind to the will of the foreign suppliers. The Taliban drug lords and their close allies like Al-Qaeda and ISIS run the opium poppy fields that are responsible for heroin among other drugs. The drug cartels from Mexico to South America are growing the coca plants responsible for cocaine and if you look, both of those areas beheadings, torture, and other ruthless psychologically sick events have become commonplace. The man in Oklahoma that beheaded a female coworker after being recruited to Islam in prison was a drug addict. So hypothetically, if years ago, drug addiction had been ruled a noncriminal medical injury illness. The Oklahoma man would have went to treatment instead of prison where he was recruited by the radical Muslims. In return, the woman in Oklahoma would still be alive! Let's look at the cost in dollars. The killer will get life in prison, and he is twenty years old. That will equate to several million dollars in court costs, appeals, and incarceration. Even if he is executed, it could take twenty years and millions of dollars. Again, a successful strike on our wallet. Even through the radical Muslim groups around the world cheer the violent murder as an American killed openly. Secretly, they are high-fiving over the financial damage we will do to ourselves as a nation. Back to the subject which started by changing addictions to a noncriminal medical problem.

Once a person becomes addicted to a drug, they do not initially want to quit. They cannot see into the future as to what they will go through or do to other people given high enough doses for a long enough period of time. It is human nature to believe the bad things will happen to other people, not you! So once an addiction is started, it is going to take some time before the person realizes that they are being physically, mentally, and financially destroyed. It is during this time that people realize they are addicted and want to stop but are not able. These addicts have good jobs responsibilities, families, goals, wants, dreams, and they for the most part are on their own. The severity of the law and impending financial destruction if they admit to being an addict forces most people to fight their addiction secretly. This is the portion of the public that would reach out to an amnesty program tied to drug rehabilitation. At this point, billions of dollars could be saved. This is where jobs and careers and families can be saved. The addicts are still taxpayers, and our nation needs that money to repair the damage the invisible war has done to the US. Without help at this point, addicts start dropping out of the workforce like flies. This is when the major damage financially starts. All the training and education that went into what they did in the workforce is wasted. Property loss due to crime starts rising. The costs in police protection go up. Court and prison costs begin to skyrocket. Remember this cost is due to laws that were tampered with by outside interests from the US. I was just making a point about addiction; it affects problems all across the *Nine-Part Recovery*

Plan, and each part of the recovery plan for the US will affect addiction. My point is we can't fix any of our problems with a single solution. For example, sending someone to rehab for addiction! Yes, that is part of the solution. But it will not cure the addiction problem by itself. Let me get a little farther into what I think will fix it. I started by labeling illegal drug imports as an act of war, and then changed the law to make addiction noncriminal. This should immediately start saving the US money on police, court, and prison costs. Next, we will have saved manpower to apply elsewhere with police, courts, and prisons. In addition, a large force of manpower will be released from prison. We will have to have a plan for them to give them purpose and something to do. Then I mentioned an amnesty program linked to rehab. The amnesty program would have to be linked to jobs, education, and financial recovery; pardons for the addicts that have a criminal record or felony status. We could use job performance, education, and financial recovery to qualify them with abstinence for pardons, an amnesty program like this only covers one-third of the addiction problem and it is the center third. In other words, one-third of the addicts are on the beginning of their addiction and don't want to quit. The other third of the addict population is in prison already. Plus the section of the population an amnesty bill would be aimed at would still try to keep their addiction secret, out of pride, or other reasons this third of the addicts whose addiction has taken hold of but they haven't lost their family or jobs yet. So in addition to amnesty linked to rehab, we would need an incentive program to tempt the imprisoned addicts to quit drugs which would be noncriminal. That's where some different types or levels of pardons should be made available. Pardoning the criminal record attached to drug related convictions and felony status would be a great incentive to keep people in prison from going back to drugs. Pardons for gun rights that have been stripped from Americans would be another valuable incentive to keep addicts from going back to drugs. There have been great efforts put forth to disarm American civilians. Just imagine some of these Muslim jihadists running through neighborhoods in the US that have no guns. In the Oklahoma beheading, thank God a civilian had a gun as the murderer was stabbing a second victim when he was shot. We were talking about pardons and amnesty along with decriminalization as the beginning steps to aid the civilian casualties that fell to addictions caused by our enemies and criminal organizations flooding our nation with drugs. The addicts that are still in the pleasure phase of their addiction will not want to quit, and the decriminalization needed to start the recovery will backup users that won't quit voluntarily. This is where we use the medical field instead of the police. Force intervention would have to be organized. This is where the displaced prison system workers could be employed by the medical field. In addition to employing displaced prison workers, a big percent of our prisons and jails could be converted to detox facilities and rehabilitation centers. This would get back a big portion of money our enemies thought we wasted on prisons. Addiction should then be declared a medical epidemic and start a national tell on your friends and loved ones to give them amnesty program. Whatever we call the program, we have to take the customers away from the suppliers. Piss test the nation if need be. Then move our military in along our southern border and use our navy to blockade the countries that the drugs are coming from. We went into Pakistan to kill Osama Bin Laden for killing 3200 Americans. Drugs have killed a lot more than 3200 people in America. So why should we not attack the manufacturing locations for the illegal drugs in the other countries? We have the most skilled military in the world. The drugs are killing people around the world so if we attacked the drug cartels, we would only be destroying the groups that are attacking the civilian population of the world. To fix this one problem or attack on America, so far it will take changing laws to decriminalize addiction, creating amnesty, and pardon programs. This will also motivate the public to turn in their loved ones for drug use and start intervention by force programs. Then mobilize our military to stop the flow of drugs into the country. This is using the military against foreign enemy intent on damaging the US not using the military against American civilians as prohibited by the Posse Comitatus Act of 1812. I mentioned this as enemy infiltrators in our government start screaming about Posse Comitatus every time someone mentions deploying our military on our border. This is a big issue in saving America. Our high-tech military mobile surveillance equipment and navy ships could put a squeeze on drug shipments like never before. This squeeze would need to come timed with the lawmakers and civilian medical personnel putting every effort into stopping addicts from using. Involve all Americans. Start a national movement to crush illegal drug sales in the US. It would be paramount to dry up the customer base in the US at the same time the military goes after drug traffickers. Drug addictions are so powerful that if we can't stop the majority of addicts from using, they will find a way to get the drugs into the US without the drug traffickers' help. If we made a significant reduction in drug use while making it very difficult and dangerous to traffic to the US, it would be perfect timing to attack and destroy illegal drug inventories no matter where they are. My thinking is if we made drug supplies short and trafficking to the US dangerous while drying up the customer base at the same time the criminal drug organizations would focus on easier places to market, what drug supplies we were not able to destroy? That would give us time to start a real education program on drug addiction as a warfare strategy to produce civilian casualties and the cost of the damage to the US. Then we could start some real scientific rehabilitation programs starting with being high on anything stronger than marijuana or alcohol being a medical emergency requiring immediate detox for immediate action. This time in our education, we educate the whole nation on how we got the addiction problem and how to stop it from happening again and how to rehabilitate the casualties. The US's economy has been attacked with drugs ever since I can remember. The late '60s was heroin then the cocaine then methamphetamine and prescriptions and here comes another wave of heroin! In all those years, the US has not come up with a successful solution to stop the imports or cure the addictions. That's hard to believe that a nation as strong and diverse as ours cannot defeat this attack tactic that is bringing the US closer toward financial ruin every year.

From my view, this backs up my observation that psyops are used to confuse, disguise, and manipulate our nation away from the answers that would put an end to it once and for all. Again I'll bring up the nine-part plan I suggested. In part three, I suggest psyops police; in part nine, I mention education of the nation;

and in part one changing our laws. They are all part of part four, decriminalizing addiction. If the whole nation was watching for psyops while we developed a true rehabilitation program for the civilian casualties caused by addiction, I believe we would immediately save the portion of our society that has been struck down with addictions. In fact, I believe our doctors and scientists have already discovered reasons and repairs for different addictions. But the same psychological warfare tactics that have stopped all the other attempts to repair our system are responsible for the continuation of the drug problem. Rehabilitation from addictive drugs would be as diverse and widespread of an operation as I laid out to stop drug trafficking to the US. So far, I have outlined law changes necessary to stop the flow of drugs into the US, and these law changes also are needed as part of a real and viable rehabilitation program for the individual addicts. Each plan and part of a plan is interconnected to the success of the whole plan. In other words, to stop drug traffic to the US, you must stop the demand. To stop the demand, you must stop the supply. To save America, we must stop the drug trafficking. To save America, we must save the addicts. If we are able to slow or stop the flow of drugs, the addicts that are released from prison will have a much better chance of not relapsing. The nation is educating itself on how our enemy infiltrated our country with drugs to bring us down financially. While watching for psyops, the doctors and scientists can have a chance of fielding a solid reliable rehabilitation program. The information is out there; it just seems that nobody has put together that several plans and programs which have to be implemented together in the proper sequence and timing; for example, drying up the supply during the decriminalization phase. Neuroscience and nutrition have taken over the stage in the search for a cure for drug addiction. Neuro-pathways as I understand is the road map of our thoughts. Neuroplasticity is the creation of new roads in the road map of our thoughts. And neurotransmitters carry the thoughts. Mental exercises are being developed by companies like Luminosity, designed specifically to enhance the development of neuroplasticity. Combine diet and nutrition in the development of good mental health and you start to have a scientific plan for recovery. The mental sides of the house connected to addictions are stress, depression, anxiety, poverty, social pressure, and being tricked or lured into addiction. Proper diet and nutrition, sunshine, fresh air, mental and physical exercise along with proper education and financial relief seem to be the components of a real recovery plan.

Now I'm not putting down the standard twelve-step programs. But the success rate in these programs is low. Connecting psychological and social to exercise and nutrition are the subjects of the education needed to heal addicts, and notify the public as to whom and why some people are more susceptible to drug warfare than others. You should be able to see how each subject that is broken or damaged is connected to all the other broken or damaged subjects that are destroying America. What that means is we have to fix all nine subjects in the *Nine-Part Recovery Plan* just to fix one part. You can see how the drug addiction recovery plan touches every other problem in our society. I haven't connected it to the IRS or taxes or big banking repairs yet. But rest assured they all connect. So far, I have touched on the illegal drug problem. The legal drug problem which is more invisible to the public affects the middle- to upper-class more unlike the illegal drug problem which affects the middle to lower class. That problem also will have to have legislative revision to crush big pharmaceutical companies which hired lobbyist and put their men in government offices and formed laws to protect them while they make profits like 570,000 percent on Xanax. Yes, that is $570,000 profit for every $1.00 they spend on material. In return, the pharmaceutical companies have their fingers in education at medical schools. There are plenty of conspiracy theorists that contend pharmaceutical companies are taking part in mind control schemes. Who knows? What I do know is that prescription drugs are being doled out instead of proper diet along with fresh air, sunshine, and exercise.

In part three and nine of the recovery plan, crime prevention would be the primary tool in stopping pharmaceutical companies from using medical education and insurance company payouts to pull off being legally the biggest drug dealer in America. All nine parts of the recovery plan affect part two of the recovery plan (counterattack), and that is to simplify the tax code. And just like the recovery plan, the tax code needs to be able to be understood by an eighth-grader. The drug trade is two of the main reasons taxes are so high. In the illegal drug trade, billions of dollars leave the US through the bottom of our economy. This money is not taxed as it would have been if it was collected by legitimate US companies. At the same time, tax dollars are being spent to try to police the illegal drug trafficking. Tax dollars are also being spent on public assistance. Tax dollars are being spent on imprisonment for drug related crimes. Tax money is being spent on new prisons. And tax revenue is being lost on the civilian population that has dropped out of the workforce. This is a primary example of damage done by an invisible war against America. So on the invisible strike using chemical warfare against the US, there is two huge tax revenue loss categories and four huge expenditure categories.

These six (6) categories affect lost or wasted tax revenue. Gross national product, property damage, medical costs, disability, and death are even bigger losses than the tax revenue. Our tax system or tax code as it is called has been under attack from all sides. The special interest groups like big banks and big businesses like pharmaceutical attack the tax code through legislation creating loopholes designed especially for them and when watchdog groups catch them and close the loopholes. The big companies hide their money overseas. Then they take their US money that they paid little or no tax on and invest it in other countries with low tax rates. The rest of the financial elite in the US hire tax attorneys and accounting firms. This leaves the middle class with a tax code so complex that the average people pay the highest rates in the nation. This is the largest part of the society. Even though the middle class pays the highest percent and encompasses the majority of the population, the rich pay over eighty percent of all taxes paid. This combination of the lower class being unable to afford to pay taxes, the middle class paying the biggest percent of their earnings, and the upper-class paying most of the tax revenue, it's a recipe for disaster. All three financial classes blame it on the government. And who is the government? "We the People!" We have been tricked, spun around, robbed, and manipulated into throwing our tax dollars away in between being robbed and cheated. Then being led to believe there is a difference between the people and the government. Once we are tricked into believing the government is enemy, the tax situation will be used to stir up dissention and chaos. The tax code has been tampered with as much as the rest of our laws by foreign enemies, organized crime, special interests, and big banking. Once the tax code was ruined, the Internal Revenue Service manned by employees competing in exceptionalism has used the tax code to destroy hardworking Americans that did not understand, interpreted unclear tax laws incorrectly, or maybe not incorrectly but in their favor. Well the IRS interprets everything in their favor. And if there is any cost they can add to your bill anywhere, they will. Their eagerness to calculate costs to be as high as possible makes an audit seem personal as if they are getting to keep for themselves everything they take from you. Now that I'm older and know more about people, I attribute their anxious piranha type traits to American exceptionalism in the workplace. The IRS collection tools and tactics given them to use on enemies of our country and blatant criminals have been misused on innocent Americans trying to start up a business in the US with a tax code that has been tampered with and manipulated so much that average Americans don't have a chance of understanding it. Well, it takes the IRS two to three years to locate new businesses that are not doing their taxes correctly. By the time interest and penalties get added to tax rates much higher than expected, it is enough to put a new business under and cause a bankruptcy. The IRS collection methods are so harsh that suicide is a common response.

For those that want to live but cannot raise the type of cash the IRS can assess against you, work under the table. This is a term used by people that work for cash only! They can't borrow from banks because of the fear of the IRS by the banks. They can't deposit in a bank account as the IRS could seize it, and you can't own any property as the IRS can seize it. For the most part, you have been stripped of any possibility of becoming financially successful. This way of doing business by the IRS has driven a large percent of Americans under the table. These people can't even use any part of the financial system that could be taxed. So this part of the population pays no tax. The US government forgives debt from other countries in addition to giving away billions in aid to poor countries. If we took a look at how many hardworking Americans have been financially destroyed by the IRS and why, we would immediately start an amnesty program to forgive tax debt for Americans back taxes. I'm not talking about criminal tax fraud. I'm talking about Americans trying to get ahead by taking side jobs, or Americans that are top of the line at what they do and try to start their own business. There are large construction companies that subcontract out work to small contractors. The big companies dangle a big dollar amount in front of men trying to get ahead, and what usually happens is the small guys don't understand the tax and insurance liability and end up owing taxes that can't be paid. Good men lose their houses and credit over taxes. They are stuck living in rental properties and working under the table jobs as the IRS uses seizure, levees, and garnishment to collect money. This money in most cases was never collected by the small business owners. There are as many tax agencies that collect from small business as you have fingers on your hand. Workman's compensation insurance is as powerful and expensive as the IRS, and independent contractors get blindsided by them all the time. The private insurance companies have hired lobbyists and got in the game also by pushing through laws requiring insurance for anything you can think of that pertains to small business. This is another prime view of the invisible war against America. If you think of all the foreign enemy that have infiltrated the government positions from county to federal, then add the money hungry special interests. You have enemy supporting the special interest who are robbing the taxpayers with laws. This has left behind a large and economically powerful group of Americans financially destroyed by the tax system, and you have the IRS keeping them from being able to recover financially. I think this is just a bonus our enemies and special interest got out of tampering with the tax laws to rob the US. This group of Americans are another disgruntled group. They are publicly shamed and that keeps them from speaking out. An amnesty bill needs to be enacted for all the tax and insurance debts due to a failed business attempt. Again, we would need all nine parts of the recovery plan to make it work. If our lawyers displaced to fix the legislative branch and the whole US was watching for psyops, the insurance companies could be made to let go of the debt small business owes for goods they did not receive. In other words, insurance companies audit small businesses just like the IRS. They calculate how much you owe by what went through your books. So without any claims or problems, they claim your owe a huge debt that the law they helped put in says you have to pay. This is why people won't try to pay these back debts. So between taxes and insurance money, small businesses didn't collect but now owe the penalties and interest; civilians feel they are being robbed! And they are, the tax code and laws are deliberately written so complexly only the thieves and manipulators that are benefiting can understand them. In order to get these groups to let go of the money owed which does not exist! It's not like someone took the money from them and won't give it back. The small business failures don't even have the money. They never had it! These people working for the IRS and other tax and insurance outfits are going to have to be put to work somewhere that benefits the US instead of damaging it. That is where simplifying the tax code helps to save our nation. There will be every big bank, big business, big government spending group, national enemy, big accounting firm, and any group with radical Muslim ties against a flat tax. The big crooks that hide within these groups and the people that want to see the US brought to its knees will be up in arms. Since there will be eight other parts of the US recovery plan (counterattack) in play that affect simplifying the tax code, I'll explain why I think we would be able to get a flat tax installed now. In part one, we are organizing and simplifying all laws. In part three, we are reorganizing crime prevention which will include psyop crime prevention units. This will be police trained in detecting CIA type tactics. In addition, the whole country will be watching our back. That will be very important because the big money behind tampering with our tax laws believe they are above the law. The billions of dollars that big business and power hungry politicians are making off the damaged tax system will have the criminal groups in full swing to stop our nation from repairing the tax system. So with the whole nation watching for psyops, we send all lawyers and prosecutors freed up by decriminalizing drug use to congress to repair and revise our laws. Fifty percent of the IRS workforce and related accounting firms and attorneys report to Internet crime units. These tens of thousands of highly paid and trained employees can be shifted over to stop Internet crime which costs billions per year. Send the IRS collection assets and their seizure, levy, and garnishment capabilities after the stolen property and money that is under attack by constant cyber-attack. With a national need to stop the horrendous loss through the Internet, the companies and employees that would be displaced by simplifying the tax code would have a great sense of purpose by moving to Internet security. This would take millions of dollars in labor that is being spent to cause billions of dollars of damage to the American workforce and spend it on a category that will save billions per year. "Internet theft." With a goal like saving America from electronic theft, we can turn American exceptionalism around. Instead of using our competitive highly skilled tax collection employees to brutalize the American workforce, send them after the criminals that have laid siege to the Internet. Let them see what American exceptionalism can do when we have pointed it in the right direction when our tax experts see that they are not going to be put out of work.

They are a force to be reckoned with, and if they don't fight simplifying the tax code with a flat tax, there will be a lot better chance of successful transition to a simple but fair inexpensive tax code. By decriminalization of addictions and amnesty with pardons to put casualties from the war against the US with drugs back to work and "paying taxes," and providing back tax forgiveness and amnesty programs for small business and struggling Americans. This will give two very large groups of Americans a chance to get back in the tax system. Both these groups would be proud to take jobs that pay taxes and bring them up from a depressed position of no hope to helping to pay our nations debts by being successful. Combine these two groups of financially salvaged Americans with reduced foreign spending and bank reform, and there will be a chance of implementing a flat tax system with a much lower rate than the average middle class pays now. If we brought the recovered addicts and the people working under the table back into the tax system, that would represent bringing a portion of poverty-stricken poor into a position to pay taxes.

This would start relieving tensions between the upper- and lower class in several ways. The rich could interoperate the self-recovery of the lower class as an effort to relieve the tax burden on the upper-class. The reduced expenses on the taxpayers by viewing addicts as medical casualties in the drug war will show up in the pockets of the rich also. And that's by way of on time rent and mortgage payments, purchase of consumer goods instead of stealing them. Then you will have the top of the line workers that were dodging the IRS by working under the table coming back into legitimate jobs. The company owners will enjoy increased productivity and less training expenses. This should show gains in tax revenue by both the new employees in the workforce and increased profit by business owners.

I don't know what a realistic rate for a flat tax would be, so I'm going to take a stab in the dark at 20 percent. With rates over 30 percent now for middle class and government bill payers saying that is not enough. That would be correct if we keep doing things the way we are. But if financial experts recalculated the financial needs of our government under the *Nine-Part Recovery Plan*, I suggest there would be hundreds of billions per year in saved tax dollars and additional tax revenue. And that's without lowering our tax rate. The total financial change with the stop of Internet theft included would be over a trillion dollars per year. This would be achieved by moving sections of the workforce from areas they are doing damage to the US to areas they are helping the US by stopping the financial damage being done to America through the invisible war. Our "counterattack" (*Nine-Part Recovery Plan*) will open the eyes of all Americans as to how and who was destroying us with our own system. So if we repair the system and operate like what we are capable and that is streamlining cost-effective operations, we should be a debt-free nation. Whether a 20 percent tax rate is a feasible starting point, it isn't the point! The point is if we continue to fix our system to where it produces more money than it spends, we could start reducing the size and operations our government is involved in. Then as the invisible weapons destroying America are destroyed, it will reduce the need for the massive government spending. That's what the whole attack on America is about. Making us spend or waste money. So if the whole country was mobilized and everybody's lights were on paying attention, maybe we could start at a 20 percent tax rate on a flat tax. That is still higher than it should be. I realize with all the years of government waste and theft, people would be ecstatic with a 20 percent tax rate. If the US ran the country cost-effectively for the last 240 years, our medical would be prepaid by government savings, and we would have no debt. That's not the case, and that is why people would be happy with a 20 percent tax rate. With modern technology and increased human knowledge, we should be able to govern ourselves cheaper each year we do it. Government programs are an open invitation for opportunists, criminals, and power seekers to pounce on them. Nobody owns them! So who cares? What happens to the money or success of the program?

If it was a private individual or contractor, they would be vigilant in protecting their agenda and property. It only makes sense to reduce the size and cost of governing. With all the special interests, organized crime, and foreign enemies throwing disinformation, distraction, illusion, and other types of deception at our government leaders and civilian population, our government is about four times the size we need. In addition to lowering taxes, we will need to work on continuously reducing the size and cost of government. That will take continuous planning on where in our society to relocate portions of the workforce to stop decline and produce revenue. While we repair the system, the business sector needs to develop competitive companies to take over inefficient government operations. If a 20 percent flat tax could be a starting point, we should be targeting 12–15 percent as a goal to move toward. I've been talking about how to bring the lower class into being productive as an incentive for bringing the classes together. There is another big financial leak in the upper-class side of the tax problem. That is the big business that sends portions of their businesses overseas to avoid taxation. Then there are the offshore accounts where money earned in the US is hidden to avoid taxation. Of course you have the mega-giants that hire lobbyists and payoff politicians to change the tax laws to suit their needs. The upper-class that employ these methods for profit are just as damaging in the lost tax revenue as the problems that plagued the lower class. This is a small percent of the wealthy that go to these extremes, but it is a tremendous amount of money. This elite portion of the upper-class uses the CIA smoke and mirrors type operations as well as foreign espionage experts to hide their money. We will need to employ persuasion and peer pressure to get financial elite noncriminals to bring their business and hidden cash back into our system. The peers of the financial elite are the upper-class. They are the ones that stick it out and pay the brunt of the US taxes each year. The peers of the financial elite are the ones that could see through the smoke and mirrors the easiest. If we were able to task our government to stop any new spending during our "counterattack" on the invisible enemy, I believe the financial elite would bring back most of the business and money they shipped overseas. If the poor started proving financially productive and lowering the need for assistance and the financial elite started bringing back work and money to the US, that would set the stage for being able to find the lowest rate that we could afford to start a flat tax at. Besides being fair, a flat tax system could be mostly automated, freeing up highly educated IRS and accounting personnel to work for Internet fraud and theft prevention teams. So with transferring a large portion of those workers to Internet theft, we get a win-win, cutting the cost of taxation and stopping theft in one move! There is another big win. With the middle class paying the highest percent of their income watching the upper-class hire accounting firms and tax attorneys to pay a lower rate than they do. It causes animosity that makes them easy targets for manipulation. So if everyone pays the same tax rate, the poor are brought into being able to pay taxes and the financial elite bring their assets back to America. Besides fixing an important part of our system, there would be relieved tensions in the class warfare potential that our enemies try to stir up. But the big one is this alleviates the potential for our enemies to manipulate disgruntled taxpayers into a revolt or being recruited by radical Muslims for terrorism. With every step in the *Nine-Part Recovery Plan (Counterattack)*, tensions should be relieved between all the groups or categories our enemies would divide us into. And with every part of the plan, more money should be saved and move prosperity and revenue generated. Part five in the recovery plan (counterattack) will also affect tax revenue dramatically. That is to fix the welfare program. Well everything I have seen the government do pertaining to welfare has made the problem worse. In the old days, welfare was handled by friends, family, and church groups. Now welfare is a multibillion dollar hole in the wallet of our nation. The welfare system is destroying the productivity of Americans as fast as the drug warfare attacks on the US. Just like any other government program, it is under attack by opportunists, special interests, and organized crime. If this is not bad enough, the program makes people lazy and destroys initiative, then creates a burden on society. It is also a ready source of votes for any politician who is willing to add more entitlements to the program. It was embarrassing to watch the Obama Administration swoop through and sprinkle money throughout the welfare system and walk off with their votes. The shameful part of it is that to the voters, it looked like the president of the US was buying votes to be reelected. But if you unravel the disinformation, clutter, smoke and mirrors, distraction, and propaganda, you would have seen a large group of Americans getting lazy and standing around waiting for another handout while the drug cartels and dealers crept up on them. If you're Al-Qaeda or Taliban and supported the drug sales to the US, you must be beside yourself with pleasure knowing you were going to get a big portion of that US government tax money while lining up casualties that will end up filling the prisons of the US at a great expense to the US in addition to the money you got for the drugs. The idleness from not having to work makes those people an easy mark for the drug dealers. So in part five of the counterattack against the invisible enemy, it says there should be a requirement for welfare and other entitlement program recipients to work at least a part-time job, minimum wage job, or volunteer job, or participate in school or education to qualify. Let me explain what I mean and what the diverse positive effects would be. Welfare is barely enough help for subsistence. If you look at what average

Americans do when they plan to move or change jobs, you will see that they have to save up money in order to be able to do it.

So how can we expect someone on welfare to be able to move or tackle a new job or career? I will throw out some ideas on how welfare could be productive instead of destructive. First thing is, we have to get the thieves, cons, opportunists, special interests, and organized crime off of the programs. It has been attacked by a school of piranha from the administrative job positions to service providers to the applicants to the organized criminals that will steal the handouts from the recipients. I would start first with the welfare department staff. Relieve them of their job duties by having them train volunteers from local groups in every part of the country. This would be the first step in a long-term plan to phase out welfare employees. To keep this generation of welfare employees employed, switch their job description to building small business entrepreneurs. Give them a mission statement of "make these people successful." Service providers for welfare recipients are scourge. These service providers are mostly built up from opportunists or criminal organizations. For the most part, the welfare organization and the service providers are pocketing a huge percent of the taxpayers' dollars allocated to welfare. So for the service providers don't think that nonprofit organizations are appropriate in an environment where charity and volunteers pave the way to help those in needs. The nonprofit designation is generally turned into a business that siphons off or misappropriates the funds that would be profit while at the same time funds an overpaid staff. What we have is a large group of people earning $70,000 a year and up, passing out $5,000–6,000 per year to recipients and all of the money comes from taxpayers. If that money is for welfare, then take the $70,000 per year the service providers get and put it back in the welfare, kitty. A good majority of services needed could be provided by the welfare recipients themselves. There are plenty of educated people and disabled professionals within the ranks of the welfare recipients. A perfect training ground for small business entrepreneurs. There is also a wealth of trained experts that are retired and willing to volunteer. Americans are compassionate and giving people. Our volunteers and charity organizations I believe would fall out to help in droves if the purpose was to reduce taxes by privatizing welfare. If we cleared the opportunists and a majority of the employees off the top of the system, the next step would be the fraud. There are foreign criminals as well as local criminals stealing millions with fake claims. If the transfer of IRS employees to Internet theft is in place, we should have a handle on stopping that loss. Then with the welfare employees transferred to small business education, entrepreneur training could begin. See how part five of the counterattack which is revamping welfare ties into the tax system repair, reorganization of crime prevention, and decriminalizing addiction, etc.

The drug cartels that target the welfare recipients as easy marks should be at bay. With decriminalization of addictions tied to amnesty and pardon programs and informants for loved ones and forced intervention programs, we should have the drug dealers off of the doorstep. There are two more precautions to take. Don't leave the welfare recipients sitting idle. Put them to work somewhere, even a disabled person can answer a phone. Education or some type of work related training should be done if there is no work available. This will take potential drug buyers off the street. In addition to keeping the welfare recipients busy, require continuous drug testing for recipients. Not to deny benefits but drug test to keep people from becoming a drug casualty in the invisible war against America. If the US adopted a policy of positive test for a dangerous illegal drug equals a medical emergency that requires immediate detox, we could start helping to get the unwilling to quit out of the supply and demand circle. Remember, the less demand, the lesser suppliers will risk a dangerous supply route.

Drug addictions are most likely the biggest reason that people are on welfare. This group once sobered up will have a lot of tradesmen and educated people. With the welfare system cleaned out of the rats, it will be time to convert welfare to small business builders. The amount a person receives on welfare is not enough to change into a productive person. Here is how I would approach the new system. We should give welfare recipients subsistence needs, require they earn money, and attend education on financial success. The problem is similar to giving a fish to a poor family. If you don't want to keep giving fish each time you see them, then you teach them how to fish. We have to approach welfare like this. It's our enemies firing all those invisible weapons at the welfare system that has kept the system broken. If we weren't being distracted, lied to, manipulated, and confused, we would see our history of how government handouts destroyed many of the American Indian tribes. Someone intervened, and several of the native groups formed corporations which are saving what's left of their tribes which were decimated with drugs and alcohol. So back to fixing welfare; we know handouts make people lazy and invite opportunists and criminals. We have to seek out people with initiative to get ahead. Reward initiative to earn extra money while on welfare. Don't cut their benefits for earning like they do now. Encourage them to have three jobs if possible or a job and school. Maybe start a business.

The more ambitious a person in bringing in money, the better benefits package they should be eligible for! The welfare benefits should be linked to financial investment and education. In other words, a 401k or IRA should be started for every welfare recipient. Financial planning for college funds for children of recipients and retirement funds. The investment planning would be a win-win in looking ahead to other problems that cause a need for welfare. That being, people with a college education are less likely to need welfare than those without it. And a lot of retirees end up on welfare. The investment accounts would be setup so every time actual money is given to a recipient, part of it goes into the investment account. Co-pay incentives should be setup to reward welfare recipients for depositing money earned from jobs or businesses they started while on welfare. As the welfare system has started from tax dollars to show part of its success, the public should see the welfare recipients pay income tax on all their jobs or businesses that they start. If we developed a flat tax system, I would assume you would be able to pay income tax at the bank as you make deposits on untaxed earned income. If everyone paid the same rate with no changing deductions, good business practice would be to pay your income tax daily if you are bringing in earned income daily. For example, if you're in a welfare small business entrepreneur program and you start a lawn service, you get paid for mowing three lawns on Monday. You should go to the bank and pay your income tax on the earned income and deposit the rest as business receivables. The welfare program should have incentives also for paying taxes like low or no interest loans. Or maybe discount equipment or services. If the welfare department had small business entrepreneurs mowing lawns, there should be businesses selling mowers, repairing mowers, sharpening blades, etc. Mutually supporting businesses would be the easiest to teach monitor and assist. Helping people to start businesses would have to be linked to teaching successful finance. To give a loan to welfare recipients to start a business would be as disastrous as free handouts. Loans attached to small business entrepreneurs in a welfare program would have to be earned through work dedication, a steady growth record, and a real lending institution willing to act as part of the financial education. The education would entail saving up to 100 percent of the amount to be borrowed and using that as collateral for the loan. The objective of the education would be to establish steady on time payments and task completion on financial matters. Daycare, lawn service, laundry service, handyman, maintenance, etc., are services that everyone on welfare could use if they were working hard to get off welfare and become successful. This group of businesses would provide in-house clients to help each other develop their businesses. There should be no restrictions on how many jobs or businesses someone could have while on welfare. A formula derived from income growth, net worth, income tax records should be the way to decide when public assistance is no longer needed.

The small business education for entrepreneurs should not be limited to residential needs around the neighborhood. Big business and trades should be invited to participate as volunteer and charity. Successful graduates from the welfare system should be asked to make small donations to the welfare system. In addition under the *Nine-Part Recovery Plan (Counterattack)*, the whole nation would be watching. We would be watching for psyops or other ways our enemies may try to disrupt our success. And while the nation is watching, they will be asked for financial donations. All the money donated to the welfare program should go to making the welfare program a private business charity. What I mean by that is that the welfare department starts its own competitive and successful businesses for profit. Its businesses should be stationed where there are welfare recipients in need of part-time or minimum wage or tradesman jobs. All profit should be invested for financial growth slated to take over welfare payments made with tax dollars. All the welfare businesses should be run at the executive level by volunteers only except for welfare recipient students in an educational position. To ensure the success of the 401k's and IRA's, they should remain under the control of the welfare department unless long-term steady increase in a person's net worth indicates the financial responsibility required to manage these types of investments. Here again, we move a large portion of our workforce from one job to another job, stopping financial damage by eliminating jobs; then reemploying the same people by creating jobs to replace the work that was damaging our society with jobs that make Americans financially successful, stops wasting tax money, and starts a new group of taxpayers producing revenue. Again, you can see how each part of the *Nine-Part Recovery Plan (Counterattack)* affects the other parts. I bring this up because if you look at the outline of the plan and read lower taxes and install a flat tax, most people would dismiss giving any thought to the possibility of lowering taxes to save America due to the enormous debt. But after explanation of each part of the plan, you see a tax waste being turned into a tax revenue producing program. That means fixing at least nine tax wastes and adding nine tax revenue incomes which makes the recovery plan plus eighteen repairs in our tax system.

This leans toward streamline cost-effective taxation. The *Nine-Part Recovery Plan* must stop waste and theft. Efficiency in the recovery plan will save money, produce tax revenue, and increase security. Each part of the plan becomes more successful with each part that achieves success. A security lapse is what allowed special interest, foreign enemies, terrorist organizations, greed, power, and organized crime to break our system and start the decline of America. Part three, reorganizing crime prevention, will touch all of the nine areas of the plan also. The infiltration and tampering with our system was done through the legislative branch. It's my belief that this is where the most important part of our broken system is. The damage from lawmaking that was manipulated by so many different influences and interests must be fixed, so all the parts of the system that are broken start working again. That makes part one of the recovery plan the starter button and part three important to enforce the repair. Legislation will be needed to empower psychological crime units. The CIA tactics that our enemies, big business, politicians, and everybody else uses everyday in America has to stop. Lying and deception must become a crime. Confusion, distraction, chaos, and clutter must be recognized as tactics. Blackmail, bribery, and terrorism are already illegal. These are some of the invisible weapons that are used to rob our nation. These tactics are also used to make laws that should be illegal as they are used to commit crimes, but the crimes cannot be prosecuted because they are protected by law. The laws that protect crime are put into law by those who are going to commit the crimes. The biggest offenders are big business, big banking, and organized crime. Some robberies and acts of profiteering are setup through a series of laws that are setup to force certain purchases from specific organizations, or make group funds like retirement savings pay for services levied against us. Private banks even gain access to profit from tax revenue. The schemes are so complicated only our most brilliant minds can find them. People were manipulated by the CIA type tactics (psyops) to put the laws in place. CIA type tactics (psyops) are used to hide the schemes with illusion, smoke screens, clutter, and deception. So we have to investigate illegal laws, cybercrime, and psyops that are used in conjunction with each other that take three different types of experts. Conspiracy is so hard to prove that they are generally referred to as theories; now these conspiracies are formed out of tampered with laws, mind games, and cyberspace. Extremely hard to find. So it is not so important to lay blame to whom and what has already happened as psyops are mostly verbal, so after the fact, they become invisible. The key is to identify them in action. That will give a criminal investigator a place to start following a crime in progress. Once a psyop tactic is spotted, it cannot only be followed but it can be backtracked by asking the proper questions before persons using psyop tactics know they are suspected. People using psyops that discover they have been detected can stop an investigation from backtracking who was involved; however, the goal of the psyop could probably be stopped.

A conspiracy that has been documented or written down could be used as a format or map to link all the parts and people together on a conspiracy that involves psyops. So parts of conspiracies are psyops. That is why they are so hard to prove. But a psyop does not have to be a conspiracy; it is part of a conspiracy. That leads me to believe conspiracy theory would be a useful tool when hunting for psyops. So when you see a psyop tactic, investigators could start comparing hypothetical conspiracies that could incorporate that specific psyop since the detection of a psyop will tell you what the objective is or was.

You will have two parts of a conspiracy if it is a conspiracy; the psyop tactics and the objective. This should be enough to theorize some different conspiracies. What would be important to an investigator at this point would be if whoever you caught employing a psyop tactic did not discover he was caught, you may be able to theorize who the other conspirators are and find evidence linking possible co-conspirators to the person employing the psyop tactic. Whereas when the person committing the psyop tactic knows he has been detected, he will not answer questions designed to connect him to other possible co-conspirators plus hide or destroy evidence that would connect conspirators. The criminal psyop police units could be manned from all types of professional displaced workers. Decriminalization of drug addiction and drying up supply and demand should supply a core of drug enforcement units already trained in deception tactics. If the CIA is reduced in size or deemed no longer necessary, that would produce another group of potential employees that could be supplemented with IRS employees and lawyers that are being displaced to improve cost-effective systems operations for the US. Psyops police should be closely linked to cyber police and legislative police. These would be three civilian categories that should work out of the same office.

There are many individual crimes being committed in these categories that have nothing to do with conspiracies, and they are destroying America also. The crimes that are being committed against the US by organized crime, foreign governments, terrorist organizations, political groups, and special interest groups fall in the conspiracy category. When these groups meet and plan to steal money of secrets, manipulate the stock market, or deceive in any way the United States or its people that is conspiring against us. Hence, forth a conspiracy is born. In the past, these groups have sacrificed individuals to keep the groups operational. This is why the same crimes keep getting committed over and over, and the only difference is there is a new "plan" (or conspiracy) each time. So I'm thinking by grouping together psyops lawmakers and cyber police, we would have a Conspiracy Division! We must catch the organized groups in their entire scope of their operations. I will address cyber police pertaining to conspiracies. The average person is not aware of the websites on the Internet that are running false information and discrediting blogs and tweets that are part of conspiracies that cross cyberspace, psyops, and laws. All the psyops techniques are used in cyberspace which is why we need cyber police to track persons responsible for psyops through cyberspace. The FBI has already started a cybercrimes section, and the NSA is deep into cyber warfare. But we need civilian crime units for everyday civilian targets. "Cyber police" that civilians can call like 911 when they are robbed, hacked, or defrauded on the Internet. In addition to instant response to cybercrime, a continuous policing not only to take down damaging websites but to track down and stop those responsible. Public education which is covered in part nine of the recovery plan (counterattack) will ensure the entire civilian population is on the lookout for psychological tactics which are responsible for hiding crime, confusing, and distracting us while we try to better America. Having the public as part of our reorganizing crime prevention will be very important in being able to stop everything or exposing it all at the same time. To get the public to be the eyes and ears in crime prevention, the relationship between the public and the police will have to be repaired. As I mentioned earlier, over the last twenty-five years, the reputation of our police officers has been destroyed. People are afraid of the police. Not so much from physical violence but from financial damage. As the police evolved from serve and protect to law enforcement, almost no one is safe from financial damage. There are so many laws, and every law can be used in several contexts. So I would say multiply our laws in the United States by four due to all the ways they can be used. I'll give an example! Recently in Washington State, my mother was ticketed for leaving the pavement with a motorized vehicle. Our police were doing "law enforcement" with no context. Well my mother who is seventy-six years old lost control on black ice, a dangerous road hazard. Thankfully, she was not injured as her vehicle rolled over and was in the ditch upside down.

Things like this have a rippling effect on respect and reputation of our police. This backs up what I was saying about almost no one being safe from the police who are doing law enforcement now. My mother has a perfectly clean police record. Her husband and two sons served honorably in the USMC. She is retired from a government nuclear job that required a security clearance. Plus she spends her spare time doing charity fund-raising. She is one of the most respected people I've known. This police officer lost his opportunity to respect and honor by not serving and protecting. This law enforcement stigma has ruined the effectiveness of our police departments everywhere. The United States needs to start a public relations education program to bring the public and police back together as public, and public service needs were intended to be. If our lawmakers reduce, revise, and organize our laws to simplify law and order. The police could stop doing law enforcement on average civilians and turn to stopping crime. Organized crime has influenced lobbyist and lawmakers into making laws that stop police from stopping crime. If we are repairing the laws, we will need the majority of our police to clean up the crime that is financially destroying America. With our police busy stopping crime and traffic control as well as law and order, law enforcement jobs would not require the highly trained police units. This would create job opportunity enforcement units that went to crime prevention; the other workers changing jobs like welfare workers, IRS, and prison staff along with rehabilitated substance abuse and poverty-stricken personnel to staff more of a meter maid type of traffic control and law and order group.

This would ease tensions in police relations. Reorganizing the police should look something like this. Traffic control units would have mobile Wi-Fi with webcams and zoom lenses. Traffic lawbreakers would have court on the spot via video conference with an adjutant or judge and be able to swipe their visa at the scene. Think of the time, manpower, and money saved. The traffic controller would have tools, gas, oil, taillights, headlights, emergency auto parts. The controller would have Internet and phone for emergency service needs. They would also be able to issue temporary license plates, tags, and insurance! See how far off target the United States has been manipulated in how and who is doing what work. Traffic control would be part of a public safety network; they would have live real-time video conferencing with hospital, doctor, and emergency room personnel. The police would have the Wi-Fi and video capabilities too. The traffic controllers could watch potential danger with their telephoto zoom and video conference it to patrolling police. Look at all the reduced tension and efficiency with a little reorganization. This would be backing the guns out of the public traffic stop. Major relief. The police would still be out in patrols just as they are now. Except they are looking for crime instead of traffic violations. Now let's add volunteer personnel to police duty. A police cruiser could hold four people. So if on patrol for public safety, the officer could take volunteers. I would organize like the military did with Combined Arms Teams (CAT teams). Difference being, you would need different things available. Instead of machine guns, anti-air missiles, and anti-tank missiles, a civilian or police CAT team would have a police officer trained in weapons and tactics, an EMT trained to save lives, legal consultant, and professional or college athlete to overpower and detain unwilling personnel by superior strength to reduce chance of injury. We could change to nonlethal use of force also. The Posse Comitatus Act was put in place in 1812 to make it illegal to use our military against our civilian population. Well, the forces that have been manipulating the police changed the way we admired and looked up to lawmen to viewing them as despised paramilitary law enforcement units that strike fear into us when we see them. The latest military surplus scandal involving giving away military armored vehicles M-16s and M-19 belt fed grenade launchers to police departments has brought to light an ever worsening problem. Posse Comitatus is being bypassed by militarizing the police. This is just another factor straining relations with the public. We can fix this in our reorganization of crime prevention with public armories where civilians control the use of military equipment. If we decriminalize drug addiction and destroy the demand through amnesty, pardons, detox, and rehabilitation and relook at the BAC of 0.08 laws, we could reset the BAC at 0.16 for DWI and require police and traffic controllers to take people with a BAC between 0.08–0.16 to their home or quarters and take addicts to medical. This would start to build a rapport between the police and the public. I believe families would start showing their appreciation and respect. Plus if the police start stopping crime at the same time that they stop destroying people and families' lives, I believe that will stop all the shooting of police officers out of revenge. That brings up the use of deadly force. The weapons and sighting systems of today are so accurate that there is little need to kill someone in most cases if our police were carrying the proper weapons and practiced nonlethal force with deadly weapons! I'll lay out a simple overview. The standard 9mm semiautomatic pistols are generally referred to as combat handguns. Part of our police manipulation to military police. They should only be used within hand to hand combat range. Other than that, there is a better weapon to use for every situation you may come across. Let me compare a few things. Any match quality rifle from 22 caliber to 308 caliber with good optics at a range of one hundred yards an average, Marine Sniper is not wondering if he can make a head shot; he is choosing the left eye or the right eye, then wondering if he is good enough to get the pupil or the white of the eye. With a 9mm pistol at twenty-five yards, one-fourth the distance, an average expert is lucky to keep all his shots in the body of a silhouette. That tells me if a police officer is going to be required to use a gun; he should have the appropriate carbine with optics and backed up with a pistol. Police in a tactical situation should have police officers in mutually supporting positions. And they should have a small caliber semiautomatic rifle with optics, a larger caliber bolt action with optics, a bean bag gun, and a tranquilizer gun available. With this combination, police should be able to bring in almost all combatants alive. Even if they are armed, a weapon is a lot smaller than an eye. Shoot their weapon first to disarm them. If our law enforcement units came out to fight crime and protect civilians, this is what it should look like. Mutually supporting teams comprised of a diverse group of experts with a wide range of weapons to pursue nonlethal tactics. Communications would include two-way telephoto video and audio with Wi-Fi monitored by psyops police, cyber police, legislative police, among other emergency first responders. The police that carry guns would change over to longer range, more accurate equipment, and add rubber bullets, bean bag bullets, Tasers, and dart guns. They would take volunteers expert in the necessities needed during an arrest.

While on patrol, they would pick up people who have had too much alcohol to risk safe operation of a vehicle and return them to their homes. They would pick up or assist drug intervention teams in taking addicts to detox. The nightly news reports would read more like this. Police patrols picked up six people operating motor vehicles after consuming too much alcohol.

They were stopped before there were any injuries or damage. They were then safely returned to their families. On the other end of town, worried parents reported what appeared to be a new drug house open for business. Police reportedly showed up with several drug intervention teams from Our Lady of Lords Hospital and escorted all infected people to the new detox center. Police boarded up the drug house and reported no additional spread of addiction. Meanwhile, gunman threatens to kill his girlfriend during an argument is disarmed and taken to jail after being treated for minor injuries. If the contacts between police and American civilians were going down more like this, everything would change. Police would be getting high-fived and patted on the back every time they showed their face in public. Not to mention the public would chip in and help them find and stop crime instead of turning their backs on it and pretending they did not see it. That is standard procedure as things are now, because of the financial disaster, left behind from all the improper laws that will be enforced. This will play a big role in part three of the recovery plan or counterattack. Part three pertains to the reorganization of law enforcement. We are being portrayed around the world as a society with a decaying moral character. This has been orchestrated by enemies and interests other than the United States. If we fixed the public relations for police, that would affect on all nine parts of the recovery plan (counterattack). We would be solidifying the repairs on our nation by bringing our people together in realization that there are many groups out to destroy us or rob us.

By working together to get out of what is destroying us–invisible warfare tactics–we will not be able to be manipulated into destroying ourselves again. By working together, we will have eyes in the back of our head along with access to every profession we need to be successful in fixing the system. In reorganizing law enforcement back into units for policing crime, this would set the standard of to "serve and protect" back in place. By adding psychological crime, cybercrime, and legislative or law crimes to policing criminals, we will achieve transparency or clarity in daily events around the nation. For example, if someone lied on a campaign advertisement, with lying being a crime, an investigation would find and charge someone in connection with the lie!

As we repair our systems, sentencing for punishment of crimes will evolve to a restorative nature. In other words, payback the cost of the damage caused by the crime. Advertisement is a multibillion dollar industry that thrives on lies and false advertisement. Imagine how much easier it would be to shop if it was illegal to lie in all parts of sales like from print on packaging to salesmen to commercials on mass media. With restorative sentencing, picture the consumer being reimbursed, the competitors being compensated, and the violator paying the investigative costs. The foreign violators could face embargoes and seizures. The attempts to clean up false advertisement in the past have been responsible for some deceptive types of advertisement that will trick you. Every CIA style trick used in espionage has been employed in advertisement. Again, with the entire nation looking for psyops, advertisers that stop short of lying but engage in trickery will start getting exposed by sharp consumers. Crime will go down, production and prosperity will go up. Taxpayers will pay less each year. Our nation's security will be majorly enhanced as our police properly organized by diversifying and working under revised and repaired laws. We'll have crime cleaned up so fast through efficiency and public support that they will be supporting homeland security in force.

Now in our recovery plan (counterattack), we are trying to save money, stop theft, increase productivity and prosperity plus increase tax revenue. So let's talk about part seven of the financial recovery plan for the US! Cutback foreign spending, redeploy overseas military assets to assist US border patrol. US backed stability by having parts of our armed forces deployed in other countries is very expensive. These countries enjoying additional security at our expense should be asked to pay the bill for it. The reasons for these deployed assets no longer exist. Illusion is used to make us waste money by the billions. We have the most mobile military in the world. We can no longer afford to be the world's police force. In addition to that, we are under attack at home. In order to stop the flow of drugs to the US, it's going to take all hands available. This is *war*! We have been manipulated into not using our troops time and time again. Deploying our troops in the US is not in violation of our constitution. It's the enemies of the US that we are trying to stop. And we are trying to stop wasting money! If the majority of our army, navy, air force, and marines are patrolling our perimeter while the demand for drugs is being dried up, that is what will keep the addiction epidemic from restarting once we stop it. The affected population will have cravings after they stop using drugs. The key to success is to cut the supply off before the population that is rehabilitating starts having cravings. The longer addicts have been without drugs, the shorter the craving period lasts and the less often they occur. So if we can make drugs hard to find, that will be the difference between success and failure in the recovery. As I mentioned before, our drug enforcement agencies are modeled after our elite commando units.

So by adding the military to the task force to keep drugs out, we are playing our A-team, something that psyops have kept from doing earlier. Let's look at the money real quick. We would cut the transportation and supply cost of having our troops overseas by having them close. The money spent by our troops would go into the local economy instead of a foreign economy. The prosperity in the local economy will produce tax revenue. Then we will have the money flowing out of the US via the drug trafficking route stopped. The organized drug cartels are responsible for most of the militarizing of our police. With the military at home for a while and civilian police practicing nonlethal use of force, that would bring us closer to trust and working together than what we are doing. Not to mention it would be more effective in our public relations and security. That brings up part six of the recovery plan–American human relations awareness. The decay of America's moral character is a target of our enemies. Although there is moral decay in the US and around the world. Examples of it are highlighted when America is the subject. Our whole country is presented as arrogant low-life. Arrogance being a key factor as to why we are being portrayed as pedophiles, criminal, and homosexuals in the news. The arrogance shows when we don't pay attention to things that are not true. Yes we have a small percent of deviance in our communities. But the majority of Americans are compassionate, accepting, hardworking, morally sound men and women of principal.

"We the People," the majority do not stand up to be counted on moral issues. We have been manipulated by political correctness. This too is your standard CIA style psyop. Yes, we tolerate and protect minorities in race, ethnicity, religion, sexuality, and other things. But there is a majority that is morally sound with upstanding principals and is being left out through a trick called political correctness. The majority is a combination of all the minorities. We can stop America from being represented by small portions or groups that do not represent mainstream American by advertising and standing up for the majority. Public awareness for human rights fits the majority. When small groups of our nation are representing us to the world news, a false interpretation of America is easy to produce. We need a national movement to stop slandering of the majority by citing individual rights. But site individual rights under human rights. Stop letting outsiders and enemies divide or categorize our population when reporting news. For example: "White cop shoots unarmed black man." This report is intended to damage the unity of the people in America. If the whole population of the US was on the lookout for psyops and human relations awareness, this report may very well have been reported as, "White Police Officer Saves Black Children from Gunman." Our nation's majority movement should focus on reporting positive events between different groups of our society.

Like when a black person helps a white person or men's groups supports women in the workforce. Maybe poverty-stricken man saves rich family from death. These are the daily actions of the majority in America.

So if our enemies and special interest groups are reporting every negative aspect of human relations in our population, then our majority should report noteworthy events between diverse categories of our population. The financial returns from stopping and repairing the continuous defacing of the American character would be felt in every part of our recovery plan by solidifying relationships of Americans working together to save America. Our security partners around the world would have renewed faith in the stability of America if it was seen publicly and in the news that all categories of Americans are working together on one plan, and we are putting a stop to dividing our people by race, religion, gender, sexuality, ethnicity, class, intellect, or any other method that is used to pit Americans against each other. The strength of our business deals with foreign and unfriendly groups would increase when outsiders see they can no longer divide us during negotiating. Dividing to conquer in our society goes beyond getting us not to support one another while outside interests separate us to run easier operations against us. But injecting conflict from every different direction and category is great for chaos, deception, and distraction. What better time to infiltrate, attack, or rob us. Solidarity in our population combined with some new education will stop further damage against our system while we repair the nine broke parts I mentioned in the recovery plan (counterattack). I suggested the simple nine-part plan and am almost through explaining how I think it would work. Now I know very complex operational orders would have to be developed for every step I suggested. But those are not needed for the general public. The public only needs an overview to see where the whole plan is going. My overview could be rewritten more sound and professional by our leaders and intellectual elites in a heartbeat. I just wanted the qualified personnel to look at the areas I believe are broken and destroying us financially. Plus I thought that some ideas not restricted by rules or individual category limit my spur new ideas for the experts. I believe the idea that several things have to be fixed at the same time just to fix one thing. I suggested a nine-part plan, but maybe the repair could be done with a six-part plan or a fifteen-part plan. I also believe that if the system was repaired or fixed that the same principals used in the repair, plan could be used to fix the rest of the system problems. It looks to me that if we fixed governing the US in a secure streamline cost-effective manner, we would be rewriting the constitution before all was said and done. This is an area that we could never approach at this time as there is a great respect and admiration for our constitution. However, if we fix our system, our nation will have to be on guard 24/7 as the 240-year-old constitution was not written to be able to withstand 21st century criminal and enemy intelligence manipulation and attack. It's held up 240 years and can be salvaged with a few repairs. In part nine of the recovery plan—modernizing the infrastructure, health, and education—the infrastructure of the US needs upgrades and repairs, and we are broke. For this reason, we should start slow by using parts of our army, navy, and corps of engineers and combining the welfare entrepreneurs and other displaced portions of the workforce. Our infrastructure should include water purification and recycling dilapidated and obsolete infrastructure by choosing portions of our military and welfare personnel that are paid with tax dollars and have a large quantity of equipment and expertise. We can select portions of the work that are primarily labor, salvage, and recycle. Start saving the money from salvage and recycle to fund future work on infrastructure. Give our recovery plan and economy a few years to save and generate money for rebuilding modern cost-effective infrastructure. The cleanup should focus on our water ways at first as that will assist the water purification efforts. Cleaning up the old rotting industry that is seeping into groundwater and the old shipyards, bridges, and debris in the water is also going to save money in the health department. Pollution cleanup is related to the infrastructure as a by-product of the industry needed to build the infrastructure. Cleaning up 240 years of by-product involves a lot of unskilled labor. A sense of purpose would accompany the unskilled labor involved in the cleanup. To me, that would translate to pride in your job. Displaced workers being given a new job is a big part of America being efficient in recovery. But producing or saving money is the purpose for displacing parts of our workforce. Although the welfare sector has a skilled portion of recipients, a large majority will be unskilled. The prison population that would be released by revised laws pertaining to drug addiction. This sector would present basically the same skill set as the welfare sector. Both of these sections of society will represent a large quantity of disabled personnel. Disabled people need to work and have responsibility not to decay further. Even if you're in a wheelchair, you can answer phones, watch gauges, file paperwork, take out trash, etc. Everyone consuming tax dollars and using infrastructure has a reason to help our nation recover. With everyone in our nation on the same plan and watching for sabotage, our charities and volunteers quite possibly could focus on donations to start up jobs in the infrastructure category. With cleanup alone, it able to take years and salvage and recycle the same. There would be billions in salvage and recycle plus the years to clean it up that would coincide with the time necessary to stop all the theft and waste while repairing the system to be a streamline cost-effective revenue producing system as it should be. So by the time the system is repaired and producing the revenue to get out of debt, the old decaying parts of the infrastructure could be cleaned up and recycled. A repaired system would have a lot of the workers that were transferred from jobs that were destroying people and production and wasting money to the damaged areas of the system that needed repairs doing repair jobs that would not be needed after the system is repaired. That's where upgrading and repairing the infrastructure comes in. The infrastructure project will create commerce and millions of jobs. This is the time to reduce dramatically the size of our government. The displaced portion of workers that repaired the system and the government workers from nonessential government offices could be absorbed by the American workforce needed to modernize our infrastructure.

During the time it takes to repair the system and prep the infrastructure, we will need to change and fulfill some educational needs that affect Americans of all ages. First, we must get the entire education industry to review what is being taught and find the false information that big business, special interests, organized crime, foreign enemies, etc., have implanted from one end of the education system to the other as a form of indoctrination or brainwashing people to believe certain customs or products are necessary education. There are two categories that need to be stressed and teaching should be started immediately; health and education! Yes, those are big subjects, but what needs to be taught is the newest science-based knowledge on health and education that has been covered up. The information that is being covered up binds health, education, money, and security together! Our health is under attack by food companies and pharmaceutical companies. The processed and amounts of cooked foods we eat slow us down and clog our bodies with chemicals, carcinogens, and other trash. So food and drug companies spend millions of dollars in advertising trickery to hide the truth in piles of false information and clutter. They even make you think they are on your side. An example, buy more fresh fruit and vegetables. Well that's better than canned which are nutritionally worthless, and they use your bodies' energy to digest them. The fresh fruits and vegetables are certainly better for you. But they are still hiding the facts because they want to sell you their product. Well, fresh fruits or veggies from the store, including organic, were picked weeks before you bought them. The nutritional value started decaying the day they were picked. So the information being hidden is we need fruits and veggies straight from the vine. This hidden information is responsible for the health care crises. In addition, two out of three of us are dying from disease caused by our diet. The pharmaceutical companies will drain as much money as they can from every American for the last twenty to thirty years of their life. Hospital and surgery bills wipe out most Americans' life savings before they die. Let's look at the rest of the connection between health, education, money, and security, diet, sunshine, fresh air, exercise; they are the components of good health. There is a type of exercise that has been hidden from the public just as the knowledge pertaining to eating food right off the vine. That is mental exercise designed to enhance memory. I have experienced two types of mental exercise. One is "KIMs" games, "Keep in Mind," and the other is Luminosity. A lazy mind is capable of thousands of percents of gain in memory capability.

The healthier you are physically, the more effective mental exercise is. In other words, the harder you work out, the faster the memory exercise will enhance your memory. This means that mental aptitude, physical fitness, and nutrition or diets are linked.

Our schools should be setup to build healthy bodies and minds. With that done in the early school years along with reading, writing, and arithmetic, our children would be one hundred percent ready for an education. Our schools should work the same way the trainers do for Olympic athletes. First, you train and then you compete. That way they are the strongest and fastest they can be during competition. Reading, writing, and arithmetic are the tools needed to learn. Our system for education does not emphasize that these must be mastered before a student can begin to learn the rest of what has to be learned. And like training the Olympian, before you send a student to his education course, train them! Proper nutrition with physical training and memory exercise will have the average student retaining one hundred percent of the education course in less time than the old methods. Now I am going to link this to money and security. Well it stands to reason that if we are stronger, smarter, and faster through proper diet, exercise, and education, we will be able to earn more money, and we will be more alert and capable to physically defend ourselves. Though this is most likely true, what I see as the connection of health and education to money and security is, one, if our nation changes our diet starting in elementary school over the course of a lifetime. The cost of dying from all the diseases related to diet will plummet. Two, by educating the public about the money saved in prescription drugs by eating fresh from the vine as often as possible instead of eating ourselves to death. The amount of money we are wasting is catastrophic. I think it is as big of a loss as the drug problem and welfare combined. So there is the connection to money, and the loss is so catastrophic that it affects the national defense budget each year. That is the connection to security. Just in our last presidency, the money wasted on the Affordable Health Care Act amounted to trillions. So much money is being wasted as the president and his staff fall prey to psychological tactics. Through their confusion and waste, we could have repaired our entire system. I see health and education as a part of our infrastructure. So what I'm getting at is indoor and outdoor gardens and terrariums in schools, public parks, grocery stores, etc. These garden fresh foods are not going to put fast food companies out of business. It's what you should eat to clean the processed food residues out of your body while getting the vitamins and minerals you need. Remember the acronym KIS or Keep It Simple. I think eating fresh from the vine is a pretty simple government plan for health care. It may take twenty years to see improvement. But it treats the problem where it starts. Just as I tried to trace the other problems back to where they start. It may very well be that some of the things we need to do are so simple that we look right past them. But regardless, our decline calls for extraordinary and historical changes. American exceptionalism has been used against us by all those who would profit or destroy us without notification with sneaky underhanded methods. It is time we turn the table and put that American exceptionalism to work repairing our system and way of life. We must open the eyes of all Americans at the same time. This observation of the decline of America should also be used by our leaders as a more realistic state of union. And more than a state of the union address. This is a call to arms! This information is for every eighth-grader up to the president of the United States of America and everyone in between. We do not even have to prove all the invisible attacks; the damage is plain enough and widespread enough to support the claims and observations I have sited. This report will take the blinders off all Americans then turn on the lights and make everyone take a look around them to see who is doing what!

This report going public will send many criminals, opportunists, blundering fools, and naive do-gooders scurrying for the dark cracks like roaches caught in the light. If we develop psychological crime units, the people using those tactics will hide or destroy evidence to tie them to crime or manipulation. A lot of leaders, bosses, executives, and politicians will be left holding the bag. The majority of these people did not know they were being used to rob and destroy our nation. In our call to arms, these people must have some clemency and be showed some compassion. Some of the people left holding the bag would be very angry to find that they were an unknowing part of a larger conspiracy. In our call to arms, we should extend out a hand to the people and let them be full patriots and finger the conspirators that made them look like a fool. What I mean by call to arms is everyone to stop all waste of gout money and stop all theft. Identify all psychological manipulation and crimes in progress. Personnel in displaced jobs categories start task organizing people and equipment to prepare for a cost-effective smooth transfer of parts of the US workforce. Investigative news personnel lend yourselves to the public and help to catch and expose some of the seriously corrupt and heinous perpetrators stealing and wasting US money. I would ask that all be news companies like FOX, CNN, NBC, CBS, ABC, the Washington Post, and the New York Times as well as all affiliated companies to run this story for the purpose of waking up the entire public at once. A recovery plan for the US decline is needed regardless of whether my proposal is looked at changed or replaced. I believe if everyone looked at this proposal, the US could come up with a doable plan to send to congress. Please, *no republicans* or *democrats*! Americans only! If a bunch of foreign enemy, organized criminals, special interest, or other groups try to use the political parties to stop us, all my words would be in vain. Remember how well the executive order worked during the Bush and Obama Presidencies! It didn't!

SUMMARY

INVISIBLE ATTACKS

#1 **Chemical Attack with Drugs**

Taliban drug lords, Mexican Cartels, along with miscellaneous organized crime groups have been infiltrated or joined by radical Muslims to attack America with drugs. This attack is an unorganized group of profiteers and jihadists all with different agendas, but the combined damage is as effective as if a military commander planned to use illegal drugs as a chemical sneak attack on the U.S.

#2   **Psychological Warfare Tactics**

CIA style strategies and tactics are being used by anyone that wants to steal something or damage someone or something in the U.S. These invisible tactics combined with the fast pace of worldwide communications have made tactics like disinformation false information persuasion, manipulation, illusion, deception, propaganda, distraction, clutter, and confusion extremely effective in tricking the masses without us knowing who did it.

#3   **Cyber Attacks**

Cyber space or the cloud is another invisible area the United States is under attack in. Visual and mental sleight of hand can be used in conjunction with every type of fraud manipulation and theft imaginable. The person involved can post these traps in space and disappear. Cyber space is also a portal to our money through electronic banking. Our money is under attack. In cyber space, military and state sponsored attacks against civilian so called soft targets are becoming common. This is also a safe route for espionage and sabotage in the form of viruses, worms, and malware which are others ways to attack our money through the cost of security and repair.

#4   **Special Interests Changing Laws**

A fracture in our system has a flood of infiltrators pouring into our Legislative Branch through the corridors of our lobbyists. For 240 years we have been adding laws to our governing system. Special Interest groups like big business, big banking, and organized crime have been setting up the people to be a captive group bound by laws that let these groups rob us or force us to buy from or to pay select special interest groups. The side effects from these thousands of laws that are only tricks to enrich a select few are financially damaging to the tax payers. They also are causing the operation of our institutions within our system to waste money cause dissention within the public and many other things that are destroying America. The technologically advanced enemies foreign governments and Muslims Jihadist type groups have followed the paths of our special interests and turned up the rate of destruction to our system and economy. Our laws have been deliberately changed and are bringing America down.

DAMAGED SYSTEMS

#5   Welfare and Entitlements

Family members, churches, and other charities took care of this problem in the past. Welfare is just like the rest of the government programs every kind of nefarious scheme to profit off this program has been pulled. Criminal executives from the top scrape money off the top by setting up lucrative services contracts for their friends. Then, organized crime is at the other end with fraudulent claims and selling drugs to idle people standing around not working. It has been well documented that handouts are destructive to humans in every way, shape, and form. The American Indians were almost completely destroyed as far as a productive group by handouts. The Alaskan Natives that are paid royalties for oil have been decimated with drugs and alcohol. Once someone gets on welfare they usually stay on it. You become lazy. Our enemies are behind growing welfare as it is destructive in so many ways. It is sad to say our leaders appear to be using the welfare group as a base of votes during elections by giving extra handouts just prior to important elections. This horrendous waste and destruction of productivity has been hidden with CIA style deception from the average American.

#6 **Health Care System**

The Affordable Health Care Act was another sample of financial destruction. A forced transfer of wealth, waste, and theft showed through the illusion that this tax to pay the crooks was to benefit the people of our nation. All the methods used in the sleight of hand was used in the behind the scenes preplanned laws to protect this theft. This was legally a very well planned theft. The laws used to set it up if left in place will cause financial damage to accrue and unproductive health gains. It appears that this is the way that President Obama's presidency was bought. The three giants behind the health care problem are the food industry, big pharmaceutical businesses, and insurance companies. These businesses were all losing out with the new information streaming out pertaining to health and nutrition. The CIA style tactics used to hide the facts that our food supply is making us sick and eating a diverse amount of fresh home-grown foods will heal us are being exposed. The pharmaceutical companies spent as much money as the food companies to cover up the truth. The whole truth is not out yet as the disinformation clutter and confusion still has a lot of people in the dark. The affordable health care act was a way to grab future financial losses back before they were taken by good health. Our enemies have infiltrated these businesses as well as they manipulate our law makers from behind the scenes.

#7   Law Enforcement and Prison System

The special interest, enemies, and organized criminals that have affected laws by using lobbyists in our law making process have scored a big win. The Sheriff's Marshalls and Deputies that used to serve and protect us are now required by law to enforce laws our enemies and special interests helped put into effect. M.A.D.D. (Mothers Against Drunk Drivers) get a lot of financial support from Muslims. It stands to reason that drug cartels and drug lords will hire law firms to hire lobbyists to support harsher drug laws in the U.S. as they do not live there. But know that they will profit more if the old addicts are jailed because they have been financially ruined. Then that makes room in their supply chain for new addicts that still have money. Those that are against us like the Muslim Jihadists are the big winners because the U.S. pages to enforce laws against drug use by Americans that they probably supplied. Then we build and staff prisons to jail the providers for the family unit that now cost the U.S. more money because they are on welfare. Plus an extra bonus when our men get out of prison they carry a felony status and will not be able to own a gun or go back to quality employment. This also is causing a riff between the public and the law enforcers that use to protect us.

#8   **Tax Code – IRS**

The special interest have snuck in so many tax breaks for the so few that it is causing the majority of tax payers to be up in arms about it. Well that's just how global enemies want us. They would like to have us as a force ready for civil war. The special interests have used CIA type strategies to hide their loop holes in 75,000 pages of laws pertaining to tax codes. Our IRS has been given the power to destroy financially to address these super thieves but laws have been manipulated to where the IRS is being used as a weapon. Politicians are using on their competition in between destroys average Americans. The IRS is so destructive you would think it was programmed by the al-Qaeda.

#9   **Education and Indoctrination**

Our people are being indoctrinated in our own education system. Grants and foundations have been used to provide books and education that teach false information so that unhealthy products may be pushed on the public by our doctors or other educators. Besides false information and propaganda being printed in text books, invisible attacks are being made through verbal lectures by teachers that have infiltrated our education system for a specific task or by a special interest. The radicalized Islamic groups are also recruiting in our schools as well as our prisons. Our enemies have blended into the civilian population and from behind the scenes are stirring up trouble. Again, the CIA style tactics are being used to cause divisions between race, gender, financial class, politics, ethnicity, and any other place conflict can be caused.

9-PART COUNTER ATTACT PLAN

#10   An Invisible Attack

An invisible attack against America using psy-ops, cyberspace, illegal drugs, and our own laws has damaged our system and turned components of our system like Law Enforcement, prisons, IRS, welfare, education and health care systems into financially wasteful organizations that are destroying America while we are being looted.

This is what a repair to our nations would look like. There are nine major problems causing the decline of America. They are all connected to or causing the problem together. So a recovery plan or counter attack will have to address and affect all nine items at the same time. Entire sections of our work force from our systems and institutions will have to be moved like players on a chess board from counterproductive or damaging jobs to cost effective productive positions.

- Move all available lawyers to Congress to reform 2-Party Politics by rewriting our laws. Abolish lobbyists and simplify the tax code.
- Write temporary laws to put into effect the recovery of America.
- Start by declaring illegal drug shipments into the U.S. an "Act of War.
- Deploy our military to our southern border. Set up naval blockades and no-fly zones against drug cartels and drug lords. Attack their supplies.
- Declare drug addiction a non-criminal medical emergency with illness and injury status.

- Release non dangerous prison population to work in medical field of drug rehabilitation and convert prison and jail space to detox and rehabilitation facilities.

- Develop amnesty and pardon programs for addicts that turn themselves in. And amnesty for those turned in by their friends or loved ones.

- Form intervention teams with police, medical and prison personnel. Drug test the nation and detox anyone using!

- Write a public relations mission statement for Law Enforcement units priorities go back to crime prevention and to serve and protect the public. Add psy-ops and cyber theft units to crime prevention for the public.

- Require welfare recipients to take a job, go to school, or start a business to be eligible for assistance. Assistance should include a 401K and or an IRA for children. Continuous drug testing that has mandatory detox and financial custodian required for active addiction.

- Ask for churches, charities, and volunteers to join the welfare department in making welfare recipients financially successful and move welfare towards the private sector and self sufficiency.

With the whole U.S. participating and watching and the nation knowing that the timing in drying up the supply of drugs while detoxing the society is key. We could cut the supply so when the addicts' cravings begin there is no supply to restart the addiction.

While the counter attack on the drug war is taking place, Congress is backed up by the law firms freed up by decriminalizing addiction could install a simple flat tax code and free up most of the IRS to join crime prevention and put the hammer down on internet theft. A pardon for honest Americans for back tax debt would bring many thousands of people working under the table into good tax paying jobs.

With law firms and IRS workers able to join the Congress bank reform would be priority in organizing, reducing, and rewriting our laws. This would stop a horrific siphon of U.S. money by select few billionaires that are taking advantage of the Federal Reserve and Fractional Reserve banking scams.

Then transparency and security could be enhanced through Awareness Education. Advertize every possible way across the nation that our enemies are stirring up conflict in our society to divide us by race, religion, gender, IQ, financial class, politics, etc.

Alert the public that CIA style tactics and strategies are being used across the board by civilians, military, and criminals to deceive us through disinformation, illusion, distraction, persuasion, manipulation, confusion, clutter, propaganda, etc.

Inform the public that our infrastructure operations have been tampered with to reduce cost effectiveness. Our education system has been breached. We are being indoctrinated with false information. A plan like this not only would stop the division of our civilian population. It would stop the division between the people and the police and the government and the people!

Maybe education could stop the deformation of character that is part of the invisible war. Let's put our sexual conduct back in the bed room and get out a little chivalry, valor, honor, and loyalty.

Printed in the USA
CPSIA information can be obtained
at www.ICGtesting.com
LVHW041450260923
759377LV00019B/176/J